# Lessons Learned

## in

# Retail Management

*While climbing the seemingly never-ending ladder of  success*

Jeannie G Bruenning

# Table of Contents

# Part 3 The Lost Art Of Customer Service

# Part 4 Personal Development

*To all that I have worked with and worked for,*

*most importantly those whom I've had the pleasure to manage*

# Introduction

My first official management position was as the General Manager for a small café located in the heart of downtown Charlotte, North Carolina. It was a new center built in hopes of drawing consumers and residents back into the city. It was appropriately named City Fair. The main entrance to this enclosed mall was the food court, and my little store was situated between the main entrance doors and the stairway that led to the retail level above. Large garage type doors lined the far side of the food court allowing for them to open during lunch hour, giving the feel that one was eating in an open air festival. These doors opened automatically when the fire alarm went off. How do I know this, you may be asking yourself? We not only served coffee, bakery items and food, we roasted our own coffee.

During the roasting process, there is a critical point when the coffee turns from roasted to burnt. Burnt coffee, however robust and rich it may be described, is just that, burnt. There is a large amount of smoke that is given off at this point, the aroma is amazing but it is frequently overpowered by the sound of the fire alarms that are triggered by its presence. At City Fair, not only did the alarms go off but the doors would rise, opening our little enclosed world to the beauty of the out of doors. After the firemen inspected the place and assured all that there was in fact nothing to be alarmed about, we would serve them coffee. The doors would once again be closed and life in City Fair would get back to normal. It was great advertisement.

It was in the late 80s and at the very beginning of the coffee craze, back when we were just beginning to educate consumers on the joy of an afternoon latte' or a morning mocha'. I was hired prior to construction on the store - and mall for that matter - being completed. By the time the store opened, I truly felt as if it was mine. I had held several positions of leadership prior to this experience, but being the General Manager was a new title for me. After being in the position for a few months, I inquired as to the reasons I had been selected. I was given two answers. The first was that I had great stories of creatively solving difficult situations. In other words, they felt I was a creative problem solver. Looking back, I understand why this would have been important, as there were a lot of problems with this young company and very few solutions. Creativity got us through each day. The second reason why I was brought on and given the title of General Manager was because I had big brown eyes, not a trait typically found on a list of desired skills. It was also an indication of the degree and type of problems needing to be solved.

It was my first real job and an education. It was my first exposure to hiring, training and terminating someone's employment. I was responsible for HR, financial, ordering, inventory, marketing and everything else that goes into running a store. About nine months in and after a two week illness that prevented me from swallowing without excruciating pain, causing me to lose almost 20 pounds, I figured out that I could not do everything; this was my first real lesson in time management. But, what that first job truly gave me was a passion for a very new and unexplored commodity called 'gourmet coffee'.

People knew about espresso but a latte' was a foreign language. I loved making espresso from the large brass ornate espresso machine, and I learned to roast and blend coffee. Green beans in brown burlap bags outlined the café. A large blue Probate roaster sat in the corner. If we weren't filling the center with the aroma of freshly roasted coffee, we were pulling hot cinnamon rolls out of the oven. It's fair to say that I learned the importance of engaging your customer's senses as a means of marketing.

Since those early years, I have worked for several companies, both in and out of the coffee world. I have hired new managers whose eyes were full of expectation and minds were swimming with new ideas. I have trained and developed managers as well as teams of people. I have terminated managers, a task that is never easy but sometimes essential. I have opened stores and closed them, scouted out new territory and opened new markets. I have had the privilege and responsibility of managing multi-unit operations. I have dusted fireplaces, scrubbed floors and cleaned bathrooms, all a vital part of the manager's role.

In the twenty some years since the late 80's, I have been fortunate to expand my management skills beyond the coffee world including; food service, retail, apparel, childcare, publishing and the interesting world of fitness. Managing is managing, the settings may change but the tasks remain the same. Within the realm of management there are two spheres, the corporate workplace and the service industry. In these two spheres, the skills may be the same but the execution is light years apart.

What creates this great divide is the customer. A corporate sales manager has the ability to pull his team aside for a discussion. He can train his new hires in the privacy of an office or cubical. He can stop the flow of interruptions and focus on the task at hand. A manager in the service industry, whether it's hospitality, food service or hard or soft line retail rarely has such a luxury. They cannot afford to stop their customer flow. Everything that is required of them to be successful in their position is done on stage in front of an audience of customers and consumers. They are the director, designer and fill the lead role. They direct their supporting cast from the stage. The curtain rarely goes down and the audience never leaves. They solve problems in the moment and ad lib their way through most of the production. A great manager can sell you tickets, man the concession stand, start the music, be on stage when the curtain rises, shake your hand on your way out and can somehow find time to fix the toilet in-between acts.

Becoming a successful Manager, whether in retail, food service, or hospitality takes time, skill and determination. Since 2008 and the change in the U.S. economy, the luxury of extra payroll hours has vanished. Managers have less staff and more work. Running their business, training staff and developing solid teams are done while providing customers with exceptional service. They are manager, worker, janitor, marketing manager and any and all other positions required that a company can no longer pay. More work and fewer employees is required to keep the doors open.

Management is no longer a job you do while you are waiting for your real job. It is not for the thin-skinned. Management is a tough job that requires great skill, personality, a sense of humor, time management, extraordinary people skills and stamina. It is a position that keeps doors open, consumers spending and companies rebuilding. It is a position of vital importance to our economy that at times offers very little appreciation or visible reward. It is one of the toughest careers one can choose – BUT if done correctly, can be one of the most rewarding careers one can ever hope to have.

Climbing the ladder of success in retail can indeed be never-ending. Companies are sold, upper management changes and with those changes come new rules, new goals. Just when you think you've arrived, someone in the real estate department hands you a list of new locations that you wouldn't recommend to your Aunt Lucy for her 1970's hat shop. But, somehow you are expected to open and run stores with stellar results. In 2008, few were able to hold on while the economy decided to take a nosedive which took most retailers on a roller coaster ride.

There is a science to most every task required as a manager. Those who take the time and effort to become great managers create an artistry that is amazing to behold. I hope that in the pages of this book, you will come to see the science of management and learn to bring your own artistry.

Manager's responsibility can be categorized in four areas: operations, people, customer service and personal development. These are the four categories that we are going to look at in this book. These are some of the lessons and perhaps secrets I've learned over the past twenty-some years. If you and I had a chance to meet prior to your first day as a manager, this is the information I would make sure you had before you ever wrote your first schedule or balanced your first register.

# Part 1

# Operations

# Operations

A true manager is a operations person. It's likely that you can't stand inline for an ice cream cone without evaluating the set up of the store, the menu board, the queue, and the kid scooping the ice cream.

Managers are operators. We walk into the grocery store and upon noticing the lines at the checkout, wait to hear the call for Joe to open his register. We notice things like empty spots on the shelves, half finished displays, missing price stickers and obscure signage. We're irritated when there's too much conversation going on behind the counter causing us to wait inline two minutes longer; or, the phone rings and the person checking us out answers it before completing our transaction.

"Wait, I'm here! I'm the person who got in my car and drove here. Why should I have to wait for that schmuck?" we shout in our heads.

Operations is the foundation of retail. Twenty years ago, we were still under the impression that retail was about *trying* things. That has changed. There have been studies done on the way we shop, what music makes us want to spend our money, and what layout forces the customer to tour our stores in a way that they will see the majority of our product. We can scientifically set up a store, play the right type of music, shine the appropriate lighting and display in a manner that draws shoppers in and makes them buy.

Operations is everything it takes to keep your store running. The parts of operations that most managers have control of are budgets, schedules, inventory, and the all important sales. Teaching someone about operations can be the easiest part of training since there is very little gray area. It is also the area that when mastered, keeps stores running smoothly and profitably. How well a manager manages operations is an art.

# Understanding Financials

Numbers tell a story. Nine times out of ten, they tell a very true story. You, as the manager, need to understand what they are saying about your operation. It doesn't matter if you work for a company who believes managers should have access to every report or not, you have to understand what the numbers you have available to you say.

If you are fortunate to work for a company who shares profit and loss statements with you, take advantage of it. Learn what each line item is and how it affects your profitability. If you don't have access to such numbers or reports, begin making up your own reports. Start with sales figures; track them, evaluate them, make notes explaining peaks and valleys. Next year, when you can't remember the snow storm that had the city shut down for three days and your sales look as if no one took the time to show up for work, your notes will explain why.

You are in business to make a profit. You, as the manager, need to understand what makes you profitable so you can operate at that level. Numbers always tell a story. It's your job to read and understand the story they are telling.

# Comps

Comps typically refers to the comparison of this year's sales to last year. This can be on a daily, weekly, monthly or quarterly basis. The goal is to always have a positive comp. Comps can be misleading. If a store is trending down year on year, a positive comp would show that the trend may be turning around – which is a good thing. However, if the year before was also a negative number, the comp percentage may not be as exciting as it appears.

Comps should also be compared to total sales. For example; on Friday, store #526 posted a 200% comp over last year. It's a great number and one that would be highlighted. HOWEVER, if that 200% was made because last year the sales were only $100 and this year they were $300 but the store really needs to do $1200 to pay the rent, then that 200% loses its impressiveness. The comp percentage should not be the only way of measuring sales because they only tell part of the story.

For new stores the comp percentage kicks in on the one year anniversary. If the first year of business was successful, then comps can be trusted to give you a clear indication on how the store is doing. If the first year was a struggle and the store did not make its budgeted sales goals, positive comps means the business is growing but may have a long way to go to be profitable.

Holidays will always mess up comp percentages. Christmas may always be December 25th, but December 25th is never on the same day or even week from year to year. When looking at comp percentages, it's important to make sure you are comparing apples to apples or in this case, holiday weeks to holiday weeks.

The goal is to consistently see increases each year. When taking over a store that is in trouble, it's much easier to post double perhaps even triple digit comps the first year. Enjoy it while it lasts as a store can't typically sustain that level of increase year after year. If a store is running successfully, it's likely that it will see up to a 10% increase year on year. That is a good steady growth.

There are extending circumstances that will affect the comp result: construction, closures of surrounding stores, mall management changes, staffing issues, and most commonly, weather. It's easy to fall into the trap of continually evaluating why people did or didn't walk into your store on any given day. Generalizations are easy to make such as, everyone is watching the game or they are all out of town, as if the entire community got in their cars and took a road trip together. If we could truly predict who and when our customers will walk into our store, we would never struggle with sales. We would always be ready for the rush and be staffed accordingly for the slow times. That doesn't happen and if it did, we would all be very successful.

There are days that for a variety of reasons, your customers didn't come in and there will be other days that it feels as if the bus pulled up and dropped everyone at your front door. Keeping notes on such occurrences will help you next year to understand why there are weeks that your sales look more like an EKG reading than a sales growth chart.

## Profitability

A business has to be profitable to stay in business. A store has to stay profitable to stay open. Profit is the amount of money left over after everything has been paid. As a manager, there are lines on the profit and loss statement that you can and can't control. For instance, you will most likely not be part of the lease agreement, thus what you pay for rent is not in your control. What you can control are: operating expenses, payroll, and sales.

## Operating Expenses

You may not be able to control every operating expense, but

there are a few that you can have a great affect on.

Store supplies can easily get out of control. Cut back on the nonessentials but never make your team go without items required to do the job. Be thrifty but don't be a scrooge. Employees should not feel they have to bring pens to the store because there are never any available.

Cleaning supplies is a line item that can be very misused. Figure out what cleaning supplies are needed and stock them, then train everyone on how to use them. You typically don't need five different products to clean the floors. Having six dusting utensils won't make people remember to dust.

Office supplies such as organization tools can be easily over budget. Keep your organizational methods simple, easy to use and easy to access.

Take time when you are placing orders for these supplies. Managers get in trouble when they don't have a system in place to track usage or need to order such supplies. When ordering - be realistic. Do you really need 12 boxes of paper clips? Sure, they are only $1.99 each but are 12 necessary? Keeping track of these items will also help you find those items that may be walking out of your store. I mentioned to a co-worker that I couldn't believe how much toilet paper my team went though. This person looked at me and then laughed, "You can't believe how many people we've terminated for stealing toilet paper," she responded. After I relayed this humorous story to my team, I noticed that the case of toilet paper we had received was lasting significantly longer.

# Inventory

If you are responsible for ordering, you have to be responsible when taking inventory. Creating order forms that are easy to read is essential. Taking the time to count supplies is a must. Setting pars will help you stay within your budget.

What is a par? A par is the amount of a particular item you need to have on hand at all times. For example, if you use 100 cups every day and you get an order once a week, you know that you must have 700 cups the beginning of your ordering week. This does not take into consideration an unexpected increase in sales or the stack of cups that accidentally falls on the floor and has to be thrown out. Eight or even 900 may be a better number to keep on hand as a par.

Creating pars requires you to track your usage over the course of several weeks. You begin by recording how much you have on hand, add to that how much you receive and at the end of the week, how much is used. Here's an example: One Wednesday you count 50 cups. You order 600 which arrive on Friday. Next Wednesday, you count 100 cups, you have used (50 + 600 = 650 – 100 = 550) 550 cups that week. The next week you do the same and find you used 700 cups, the following week 600 cups and the next week 675. To find the average, you will add 550 +700+600+675=2525. Divide 2525 by the four weeks and the average usage is 632 cups. Remember those story problems in third grade? Who would have thought?

Now you must get the calendar involved. You are looking for anything that may increase or greatly decrease your business. What events are happening in the upcoming week? What are your sales projections for the next weeks? Is next week going to be an average week (or a 632 cup week) or is there a parade scheduled to go past your store and you'll most likely see an increase in traffic? In fact, last year on this same event you doubled your business; so no, 632 cups in not going to be sufficient.

You will need to adjust your pars as your business changes. If your business is growing rapidly, you will be increasing your pars regularly. The par gives you a starting point. If your business is going through a negative trend and you don't make adjustments to the pars, you'll soon have a backroom full of cups.

Setting pars and taking inventory is vital in running a profitable store. I had just taken over a very busy store that had very few systems in place. As I began to tackle the weekly inventory and ordering, I quickly realized that there were items we were ordering in an enormous amount. After a few weeks of tracking our inventory vs. our sales of such items, it was apparent that half of the amount received was not being sold, yet it was not on the shelves. *Hmmm, there seems to be another problem*, I quickly realized.

Unfortunately, I didn't realize the enormity of the problem.

The staff was in the habit of stocking their own shelves with product from the store. This behavior did not stop with items they could shove into their backpacks, it carried over into food they would order but never saw the need to pay. For some, they were eating three meals a day for free, on and off the clock. With the amount of product missing each week, I assumed they were not only feeding themselves but many were enjoying the bounty.

Within a month, I had inventory and the 'help yourself' issues under control. By month two the store was showing an increase in profitability even though sales were not yet increasing. By the end of the first quarter, the store was showing huge increases to the bottom line. All because we were taking inventory, creating pars and ordering correctly.

## Payroll

Payroll is usually the largest expense and the one that managers may feel the least in control. Although a manager may not be the one setting starting pay rate, deciding which benefits a company is going to offer, or determining local government work requirements, a manager can control overstaffing, balancing full time and part time employees, and most importantly assuring that everyone is doing the job they were hired to do. These are all factors that impact payroll.

The first step into making sure payroll budgets are met is in writing the schedule. Whether your company tracks payroll hours or payroll dollars, there should be equations created to assist a manager in creating a schedule. Before you ever put a name on the schedule, take time to evaluate it.

- How many hours do you have for scheduling?

- How many hours are needed to cover just the basic work week?

- How many hours are left over and where should they be used? When are the busiest times of the day?

- What is your busiest day?

If your store is open from 10:00am to 9:00pm seven days a week, that equals 77 hours. How much time does it take to open and close your store? Let's say a half hour on either side is sufficient. This adds another seven hours to the schedule making it 84 hours for one person coverage. If you have two person coverage, now we are at 168 hours. Figure in lunches, breaks and employee work laws and that number quickly grows. I've seen many examples of companies who give managers a specific amount of hours to schedule and when those hours are actually graphed out, are not sufficient to cover the hours of operation. You need to understand how many hours are required just to have the doors open, cover breaks and meet your state's employment laws. Then you begin building the schedule to meet the needs of your business.

Managers will typically put their best people on the busiest times of the day or days of the week. Thus, those days and times continue to be the busiest. This is great for maintaining sales but it does little to grow them.

Example: Store #265 sales report shows that 55% of their business is done between 2:00p.m.-6:00p.m. 3% is done from 6:00p.m.-close and 42% is done before 2:00p.m. The manager scheduled one person until 1:00p.m., 2 people 2:00p.m.-6:00p.m. and 2 people to close. The trend stayed the same.

A new manager came in and spent time looking at the numbers in hope of figuring out the story. She realized that 42% of the business may happen before 2:00p.m. but 80% of that happened from 11:00a.m.-1:00p.m. When she pulled out those two hours, they became the busiest two hours of the day. She added an additional person at 11:00a.m. and sales quickly rose to 48% of the day's business. Within a few months, the store had increased sales – not just moved them around – business now was a 50% split between the two day parts.

So what do you do with the nights? If you are in a location where the nights are slow, this should be project time, especially if you are required to have more than one person to close. If your store is in a secure location and closing with one person is allowed, do it. And as a manager, schedule yourself to work several of those nights. You'll be amazed how much manager work you can get done when you are all alone in your store and there's no one to manage but yourself. However, never

ever take chances on the safety of your team members to save payroll hours by having one person close or open alone.

If you are required to have more people than your business demands – use a nightly check list. Have your team brainstorm as to which and how many tasks need to be moved to the night. You may find you need less people during the day when doing this. We usually fill our mornings with projects and keep the cleaning to the night crew. Turn that around. If you clean the bathroom once a day, clean it at 11:00am or 2:00 in the afternoon. Why should the first customers of the day be the only ones to use a freshly cleaned restroom? Let the night crew take on projects that are eating up selling time so your sales people can focus on selling when there are actually customers in the store. You may find you need less people to close and are able to keep the daytime staff busy.

The easy and sure way to hit your payroll hours is to write a schedule that is five hours less than what you are allowed. It's easier to shave five hours off a week's schedule than to try to cut them the end of the week because you are over in hours.

If you can increase your sales by increasing your hours – do it! I give you my permission, but remember, you will have to answer for it. When running a store, I am notorious for going over in hours. I am also notorious for posting 30 – 50% sales increases on a consistent basis. You can't grow sales without sales people, and you can't have the right people in the right places without taking the time to plan. Analyze the numbers, map out a perfect schedule and make decisions that will grow your business. It all starts with writing a solid schedule.

Scheduling is as essential to the success of your business as is unlocking the door every morning. The schedule is the tool used which tells your team when and what hours of their lives they will be giving to you. Time is as important as money. The degree that a manager respects the time of his employees is the degree of respect he has for them.

Scheduling should not be done quickly or taken lightly. It should be done at least 3 weeks in advance if not more. Managers who write a schedule one week at a time are always behind the eight-ball. They deal with schedule changes, availability issues, conflicts and call offs. Talk to their team and you will quickly see that the level of respect they have for their 'never on top of it' manager equals the manager's respect of their time and lives. Find a team who has a schedule written at least 3 weeks in advance, they love their manager, they take on the responsibility to find their own replacement, they feel as if they have a life outside of work and that, in and of itself, boosts their appreciation for their job and their hours. They feel respected. Such an easy way to make a team feel as if their manager really cares about them.

It's as simple as that. Time is money. A manager who does not respect her team's time is in many ways robbing them.

# Secrets to Scheduling

Have a 'request off calendar' where everyone writes in their requests off. If there are times that requests are blacked out – black them out. This is retail; it comes with weekends, holidays and nights. If you don't like working them, don't work retail.

Make it known that once the schedule is written, it is their responsibility to fill shifts they are unable to fill. You can do this when you post a schedule 3 to 4 weeks out. You CAN'T do it if you're writing a schedule on Friday for Monday – it's not fair. You have to get your shit together before you can expect it of your team. Don't be a drill sergeant either, as there will be unexpected situations where people need time off, and your ability and willingness to assist them is another way of showing your concern and appreciation of them.

Hours are earned, not guaranteed. A great manager has enough staff which allows him to avoid having a warm body on the schedule. Warm bodies turn cold quickly. Your top sellers, top performers, most responsible, multi-taskers; the people you can't do without – get the hours!!! If you want hours, be a top performer, top seller, and responsible. The schedule equals hours and hours equals dollars. I can reward your hard work with money by giving you hours. If you suck, you're not going to get hours. If you need hours, then be a responsible employee and I'll give you everything you need.

We can't leave scheduling without addressing one very important element, your team. You will undoubtedly have employees with different levels of ability. Leveraging those abilities will help you schedule them at times when the business requires it. You'll want the person who can process shipments quickly on days when large orders arrive. It would be foolish not to schedule your visual merchandising expert on the day you have to change the floor. That makes sense, its smart business.

It becomes a problem when there are only a few on the team that *can get the job done.* If you find yourself fearful to leave certain employees unattended, there is a bigger issue. If Kathy fails to follow through with tasks or Sue has to be watched constantly, you need to take a closer look and address the performance issues quickly. Most schedules don't have a line for "those who we pay just because they show up for work". In a large or small staff, everyone needs to bring something to the table. What they bring will vary, but bringing something is essential. When writing the schedule, you are responsible to schedule these skills according to the needs of your business.

The schedule is vital to all operations. Manage it that way. Make it important. It should be a priority on your list. It must be done well in advance. It, after all, represents $$$ and $$$ talks.

# Sales

Sales solve every problem and cover a multitude of sins. With increased sales come increased budgets, more staff and rewards. No one really cares if you overspend a little in payroll if sales go through the roof. Sales make profit; sales keep the doors open and pay your salary.

Sales require the three P's; People, Product and Placement. You can have bad product, but if you make it look great and have amazing people, you'll be successful. You can have great product with not so great placement but have great sales people and you'll be successful. You can have the most amazing product, spend zillions on placement but if your people suck – so will your sales.

People are the key to sales. Your team will make you or break you when it comes to reaching your sales goals. You are responsible for building your team – thus you are responsible for your sales. If your people are not producing what you need them to, take it seriously. Train them, coach them and if need be, replace them. If you are not hitting sales - you're not doing the job you were hired to do. Without sales there is no store, no team and no paycheck.

Product is important. Know it, understand it and train your team. Placement, make it look good. Keep your store clean and easy to shop. Move stuff around. Know your inventory. If you find that you have too much of one thing, make it look amazing and watch it start to sell. Customer Service is essential. Every display must be evaluated from the customer's perspective.

Hire sales people! Not everyone can sell, it is a skill. You can train someone to sell but there is no substituting for someone who is a natural sales person. You'll know it immediately. They are the ones that when given a sales goal, can barely contain their excitement. When you find these people, leverage their gift. Don't bog them down with tasks that take them from the selling floor. There are very few sales people who can do both tasks and sell at the same time. Tasks are easy, you can hire and train almost anyone to complete tasks. Finding strong sales people is not so easy.

We typically don't honor our sales people as we should. We promote the people who get the tasks done. We find the ones with management skills to become our key holders and manage shifts. I have met very few great managers who are also great sales people. They are two very different skill sets. It is important to let your sales people know how very important they are to your team.

I hired a woman who had retired from her administrative job and was trying her hand at retail. She found that she really enjoyed selling and she was successful at it. During a conversation, I expressed my admiration for sales people, I can sell but I've had to learn how. I told her how important sales people are to the team. "I can hire anyone and teach them how to use the register, but finding great sales people is not so easy," I said. "I would rather hire someone to stand at that register and ring all day, if it allows employees such as yourself to be free to take care of customers and sell our product."

In a world where those who are task oriented get the promotion, we have to find ways to show appreciation to those who can make sales. After all, if it weren't for the sales, we wouldn't have tasks to manage.

Sales don't just matter – they are everything.

Companies manage sales goals differently. Some focus on an hourly sale goal, some on a daily goal. There are those who work with individual sales goals. In all my experience, I prefer a team goal rather than individual. It's a basic math equation. If the daily goal is $2,500 and there are five people scheduled, an individual sales goal would give each employee a $500 goal. Take that same team of five and ask them to work on a team goal of $2,500, now you have 5 people focused on $2,500 and the sky is the limit.

I heard one employee say, "my goal's in, I'm done for the day." Individual goals can limit people's potential. A barista doesn't say, "I've made 200 lattes today, I'm done." He makes as many lattes as are ordered. Sales people need to make as many sales as the day allows even if it surpasses their goal.

I love sales contests, but only when they are fair to all those participating. If Sue works the busiest part of the day and John works nights, which are less than 10% of the days sales, Sue will most likely win every sales contest unless the managers makes it a fair playing field.

Too many contests can lose impact. Keep them simple, keep them fair. Make sure the contest is trackable and easy to see the results. Announce the winner in a timely fashion and if there is a reward, pay it out as quickly as possible. Contests with delayed gratification are never a good thing.

# Backroom Secrets

A Backroom is full of secrets. Movies could be made, books could be written on the adventures of some backrooms. The Backroom is much more than the space provided for storage, the Backroom is a snapshot of the overall operations of a business.

Many managers fight this generalization; these are the same managers who find lots of excuses for underachieving staffs, missing sales goals and the inability to meet deadlines. The Backroom is the staff's private quarters; its cleanliness, organization and layout cannot be blamed on messy customers. It is the sole responsibility of the staff.

Backrooms are not high priority for any store design. Money is not made out of the backroom, thus they are the left-over space. They are the evil necessity for most store designs. Thus, the backroom is typically small and shapeless. If the business is related to food service, there will be sinks, refrigerators, water heaters, ice makers and a handful of other required pieces of equipment. In most locations, these are not always placed conveniently. They are also difficult or impossible to move.

The Backroom serves as the holding areas for seasonal merchandise. In all retail locations, the Backroom will be in a continual state of flux throughout the year. Merchandise is never the same size and rarely comes in identical sized boxes.

So what does the Backroom say about a store?

## Cleanliness = Respect

Keeping the Backroom clean takes extra effort. It is only seen and used by the team. Thus, the extra effort is only seen by team members. The cleanliness of the Backroom is a measurable level of respect of the team for each other.

If it is a Backroom of a food establishment, it is also an indication of respect for the customer. The question must be asked, if the customer were to take a tour of the backroom, would they eat at your location? If not, it is a clear indication that the team does not respect the rules for food safety. The customer trusts that their meals are being prepared in a clean work environment by fellow team members.

# Organization = The Ability to Prioritize

Managers who find it difficult to organize their time and responsibility, also have a difficult time organizing a backroom. What item stored in the Backroom is the number one item the team has to come back for? Where is this item located? Is it in the back corner? Does it require a ladder because it's on the top shelf? The most used items need to be easily accessible. If your business requires taking regular inventory and placing orders, is the Backroom set up to accomplish these tasks easily?

Holidays are always crazy in a backroom; extra merchandise, odd shaped displays and extra packaging. As the Backroom begins to empty, is it being reorganized?

# Manager's Work Space Says It All

The manager's workspace is a reflection of their organizational skills and what they believe is priority. A training manager will have checklists, calendars, reports and a multitude of other forms filling the walls. A cluttered desk is a sign of being unorganized; it can also be a sign of the team's lack of respect for the manager's responsibility. The notes and signs around the workspace speaks volumes to the manager's ability to communicate. Signs such as: THIS IS MY WORKSPACE – STAY AWAY reveal a manager who has not earned respect but has to shout for it even if it's on paper.

# Broken Equipment = Self Esteem

"It's been broken for awhile; we've just learned to use it broken." This is the martyr syndrome. What's really being said is, "We aren't important enough to get it fixed or afford a new one." A team member who is always having to 'make it work' quickly learns that they are not important enough to be given tools that work. This attitude is quickly relayed to the customer.

# Backroom is the Hangout = Lack of Customer Service

When the Backroom becomes the hangout, a team has lost, or may never have understood, customer service. The Backroom is there to support the business, not escape from it. The Backroom does not generate income; customers don't shop the backroom. They also cannot be helped on the floor if everyone is in the backroom. Most importantly, a manager cannot have a true understanding of their business if they are spending the majority of their time in the backroom.

I've visited many backrooms. No two are ever the same. The Backroom is a vital part of a business. It also is a snapshot of the overall operations of a business. On more than one occasion as I've watched an entire staff entering the Backroom for a multitude of reasons, I couldn't help but ask, "If we are all in the backroom – who's taking care of the customer?"

# Backroom Cleanliness

Let's take a tour of your backroom. The Backroom is a work in progress. As you begin to make your list of things needing to be cleaned, fixed or rearranged, you will also need to prioritize the time, payroll and effort needed to get the Backroom in order. This may be a long-term task, but it is a task that cannot be ignored.

- Look in the corners and under the shelves.

- Make your list of what needs immediate attention and what may need additional equipment.

- Burned out lights can make a Backroom dark and seemingly dirty.

- Floors need to be mopped, bathrooms cleaned and shelves dusted.

## Backroom Organization

- What is the most required item stored in the backroom? Where is it located? Where should it be?

- Is there leftover holiday merchandise? What are you going to do with it?

- Is there broken or returnable merchandise hanging around? What will it take to get rid of it?

# Backroom Manager's Workspace

- Does this area reflect the way you approach your job?

- What does it say to the team?

- Is it organized in such a way to allow you to work more efficiently or is the workspace filled with clutter? Are there old files stacked on shelves?

- What is trash and what is important?

# Backroom Broken Equipment

- If you can't return it or fix it – trash it!

- If it's been hanging around for more than 90 days – it's not needed.

# Backroom Hangout

Finding out what really happens in the Backroom may be difficult unless someone is willing to confess. Be very aware when you enter the store, whether for a shift or an unexpected visit, if several of the staff exit the backroom, it's a clue that they are spending more time back there than necessary.

After paying close attention to your backroom, what does it say about the operation of your business?

Set in place a plan to clean, organize and set a new standard for your backroom. This may take several weeks to accomplish, but once it is done, you will see a difference in your team and your sales.

# Prioritizing

A manager cannot possibly perform every responsibility on their job description in an average work week. It is mathematically impossible. Don't believe it? Attach the amount of time it takes to do each task on your "to do" list for this week, don't forget to add in the amount of time required on the selling floor. If the total fits into a normal work week – KEEP YOUR JOB! For most, it will not. Successful managers manage the tasks – they don't do all of them.

Prioritizing can be challenging, especially for someone who is not naturally organized or someone who struggles with being a perfectionist. Prioritizing is an essential part of management.

# How to Prioritize

Make a list of the responsibilities as defined by your job description. Your list should be somewhere between 8 to 20 tasks. Here are some examples:

- Interviewing/Hiring

- Training

- Deposits

- Ordering

- Inventory

- Payroll reporting and adjusting

- Marketing

- Company Directives / Plan-o-grams / Merchandising

- Markdowns

- Attending Manager Meetings

- Scheduling

- One on ones with staff

Once your list is complete, copy them onto index cards, one task per card. Now, put the cards in order of importance. There are no wrong orders. If you were in a group of fellow managers, each manager would have a different list of importance. Once they are in order, take some time to look at them. Their order speaks volumes as to how you approach your job. In many cases, it could also shine some insight into conflicts you could be experiencing with your boss. For instance, if you place Company Directives at the bottom half of your list, you are likely not concerned about deadlines for putting such directives into play. Your boss, on the other hand, may feel that by not implementing directives quickly shows a lack of interest and commitment on your behalf. Seeing how you prioritize your job description will shine a light on how you approach your job.

After you have your tasks in order, look at them again and ask, "What would my boss say are the most important tasks?" Do you need to make some changes? These need to go at the top of the list.

Now that they are in order, select the tasks that are exclusive to the position of manager. Again, this is usually dictated by your company. Managers usually are solely responsible for tasks such as adjusting payroll, hiring, one on ones and even inventory.

To this list of exclusive tasks, add one task that remains on the list that you love to do. The smaller list that you now have should be no longer than six tasks. If you have more than six, look again, you need to pull something out.

This new list of tasks is your new job description. You are solely responsible for these tasks. What are you going to do with the tasks that remain? You are going to delegate them to your team. Not only does this exercise help you prioritize your tasks, it provides you with tasks to assist in training and development.

I did this exercise at a manager's meeting. Sixteen managers were all given the same cards listing the same tasks. After they were asked to prioritize their list, 16 managers sat in front of me with 16 different lists. It was an exercise in understanding each other and the diversity of our team. After I instructed them to pick out the six tasks that only they could do, I asked, "What's left?" One manager looked down at her list. She then looked up at me. She knew where I was going. She knew we were going to start talking about delegating. With a smile on her face, she said, "I hate you!" I laughed and so did she. She didn't do well with delegating.

There is an old saying that the great manager is the one standing in the corner with a broom and dustpan because her team is doing everything else. The better example is that the successful manager is the one on the selling floor providing his customers with exemplary customer service, interacting with his team, and driving sales through the roof, while his team is actively engaged in the daily responsibilities of the business.

A manager who has mastered the skill of prioritizing tasks always finds the time to complete them. The manager who does not, finds lots of excuses.

I recall standing at a three compartment sink one day finishing up the lunch dishes as my boss walked behind me. As he passed, he said, "You are a very expensive dishwasher." Those seven words have stuck with me. When you find yourself doing tasks that someone else really should be doing, tell yourself, "I am a very expensive _____." This is not to say that managers are above washing dishes, dusting or cleaning the toilet. However, if you are doing it because no one else will do it or you have failed to assign someone to the task, then the words fit. You have far too much to do to make your store successful to be wasting time doing tasks that should be on a checklist or delegated to your team members.

# Delegating

We've all been given tasks to do without being trained how to do them. Don't be a 'oh just figure it out' kind of manager. When delegating tasks, make sure the person who is taking on this new responsibility understands what they are expected to do and even more, how to do it. The more focus you put on instructing them, the more importance they will put on the task. Tasks that are 'oh, just figure it out' aren't important, thus little effort will be given to them. You will always get out what you put in.

When you are delegating, make sure the task fits the skill set of the person you have in mind for the task. Easy tasks are a great way to get new hires engaged in the business. Difficult tasks are a stamp of approval. Whether you are aware of it or not, the team is evaluating every task delegated. They have a preconceived pecking order of responsibilities.

Delegating is also a great time to have conversations with underperformers. An underperforming employee should not be given a significant task in hopes that they will prove themselves. If they are an underperformer, they have to prove they are able to perform daily tasks before they are trusted with more. It is likely that you will be questioned by your underperformers as to why they were not chosen. Use this opportunity for an honest conversation. Tell them what you need to see out of them. Give them real examples of how they need to improve. Honest conversations are much easier to have when they drop in your lap.

After you have clearly communicated the task and trained or made sure that they have the training material needed for that task – this is not simply pointing to the operation manual – follow up. Check on them during the process. Ask how they are doing. Make sure they know they can ask for assistance. When the task is complete, inspect it! Nothing worse than accomplishing a task and no one gives a rip when it's done. This is a great time to announce to the team that Steve is now the expert on color coding. Steve feels validated and the team is well aware that he was successful. A strong manager would then assign Steve the task of training at least one other person on the task. Such a simple and effortless way to give Steve your approval.

# Setting Goals

The mind doesn't decipher between reality and fiction. It processes both in the same way. A child has to be taught what fiction is; to him the Transformer on the TV screen is as real as the kid next door. When I set a goal for myself, my mind processes it as if it is reality. When I take that goal seriously, my mind begins to act as if that particular goal has already been achieved. This is why positive affirmation is credited for making things happen. It's not that the mind is creating the result; it's that the mind is working as if the result hoped for is reality.

# Here's an example:

The goal is to be healthy. I begin to tell myself that I am healthy. My mind believes me when I say, "I am healthy" and begins to think in ways of maintaining health. It will not stop me from avoiding the gym or force me to put down the cookies. It will, however, send me messages that those things are not healthy. It will also guide me to things that will make me healthy. My mind should be working for me not against me.

Goals come with varying degrees of achievability. A college student can set a goal of living independently. This can happen in a variety of ways:

• Move out of mom and dad's house.

• Have my own apartment.

• Buy a house.


All three statements achieve the same goal – independence. But, each comes with a different degree of achievability.

• Moving out of mom and dad's house can be easily attained in several ways: roommates, housemates, campus life, etc.

• Having an apartment comes with a much larger price tag and will most likely take more time.

• Buying a house will most certainly give independence, but

the price, commitment level and achievability changes greatly.

When setting goals, it is important to understand what you want the end result to look like and state your goal in the manner you want to achieve it.

In business, goal setting is what drives us, it also helps to keep us accountable, and it most certainly assists in allowing us to achieve much more than those who simply show up for work.

Let's set goals in different areas of our business: financial, staffing, training & development, marketing, store performance, holiday and most importantly, personal development.

When setting goals, there needs to be varying degrees of achievability: move out, apartment or house. If all of our goals are houses, we'll quit the game early feeling very defeated. If all our goals are simply to move out, we'll never be really challenged – great managers love the challenge.

Goals also need to be adjustable. Your sales may be right on track until that large tree that stands in the middle of your parking lot decides to take a tumble and no one can get to your location. It doesn't matter how many positive affirmations you say, your business will be affected.

# Rules for Setting Goals:

Define the end result before setting the goal: we will be 2% under payroll while maintaining proper staffing levels. It's easy to come in under budget when you don't have anyone working.

Have varying degrees of achievability; if they are all easy, it's not a goal. If every goal demands great effort, it's likely that none will be achieved.

Write them down and visit them often. Make your mind work for you opposed to the other way around. You state your goal enough times and your mind will respond as if it has already happened.

Let's get started!

# Goal Setting – Financials

• What percentage over budget do you want to achieve in sales?

• What percentage under budget do you want to achieve in payroll?

• What percentage of this year's increase do you want to see go to the bottom line?

• Pick a line item on your P&L that you don't understand.

Make it a goal to understand and control that line item by the end of the year.

## Goal Setting - Staffing

• Take time to evaluate your current staffing levels. Are they what you need?

• Do you have the right amount of people in place to meet the demands of the business? What adjustments do you need to make?

• Set a goal that you will never find yourself understaffed this year.

• Set a goal for the number of interviews you will do each month, whether you hire people or not.

• Does your company have a turnover percentage? If so, set a goal to be under that percentage. Excellent manager's hire great people and turnover should always be below the company average.

## Goals Setting - Training & Development

• Do you have someone who should be promoted? If so, set a goal when you will have them ready for the next level.

• How knowledgeable is your team about the business?
What are you going to do to fix that?

• Are you a training manager? Do you want to be known as
that? Set a goal that your business will maintain such high
levels of excellence that you become the go-to-person!

GET YOUR TEAM INVOLVED! Ask each employee what part
of the business do they want to learn more about? Your goal
is to teach them. If someone responds that they don't want to
know anymore – set a goal as to when you will replace them!

## Goals Setting - Store Performance

• What do you want your store to be known for? What will it
take for you to get there?

## Goals Setting - Marketing

• Most businesses cannot depend completely on the sales
within their four walls – what are your marketing options
and how are you going to achieve them?

• This is as simple as committing to doing one event a month
outside your store and can be as extreme as increasing sales

by 5% through outside marketing and events.

# Goals Setting - Personal Development

*Now it's time to get personal.*

- What improvements do you want to make this year?

- As a manager, what do you want to be known for?

- Are you balancing work and home life? What needs to change?

- Is it time for a new position inside or outside the company? When does that need to happen?

- Is there one thing on your "Someday" list that you can make happen this year? Let's make it happen!

# Goal Setting – Holiday

- What worked or didn't work when setting up for holiday this year?

- What is the one thing you will do differently next year?

- Were your staffing levels appropriate? How many employees will you need next year?

- Did you have enough product? Did you have too much? How will you control it better in this year?

• Did you achieve your sales goals? What percentage increase do you want to achieve this year?

• Were you able to manage the amount of hours required of you? What do you want the next Holiday to look like as far as your schedule?

Find a notebook and write across the front: Goals. Keep it handy and refer to it often. It will become your personal manager.

# Excellence vs. The Best

After winning a sales contest, I had the privilege of attending a dinner with two other winning managers and our CEO. During dinner, he asked each of us if we knew we were going to win before the contest even started? Great question, I thought. The first manager told of her game plan to get everyone motivated before the contest began and all she had done to make sure they were on top. The second manager spoke about the goal charts they had and how they tracked the sales all day long throughout the contest. When it was my turn I simply said, "We were determined to be excellent."

Excellence doesn't always mean the top performer or the biggest sales. It doesn't guarantee triple digit positive comps.

Excellence does mean that everyone on the team gave 100% and did the best they could do. Striving for excellence is not stressful, striving to be the best is stressful. Striving for Excellence brings consistency, it smoothes out the highs and the lows.

Many years after that dinner and after seeing a report that had listed my store in the running for a contest, I asked my assistant, "What contest are we winning now?"

She laughed and said, "The holiday one. You know, the one I showed you, and you said that you've never won a contest that you set out to win. So we just set it aside."

I laughed, nodded my head and said, "Nope, I've never won a contest I set out to win. Good thing we weren't trying."

"What will you say when they ask how you won this one?" I shrugged my shoulders. It was the fifth contest we had won that year.

Excellence doesn't always mean you win. It means that you are the best of the best. It doesn't guarantee the grand prize. It will mean that your team will give 100% and at the end of the day, each one will be proud of what was accomplished.

# Fixing Stores That Are In Trouble

My career has been filled with taking over stores in trouble and turning them around. Early in my career I just assumed anyone could do that, after all, isn't that what managers do? I came to realize that it's not all that simple for most. Taking over a store in trouble is definitely hard work, but it is also very rewarding. It should not take a year to do so. When a store is at the bottom, the only way to go is up. The first year is full of record breaking comps, what more could one ask?

I believe a manager needs to hit the ground running when they take over a troubled store. They need a plan and they need to be ready for 90 days of hard work. Yep, 90 days! I know that stores can be turned around in 90 days. Even if you have a location challenged store, you may not be able to turn it completely around, but you will see improvement in three months.

The following is how it's done. If you are the manager taking over a struggling location, or if you are experiencing a negative year and year trend and are sick of it, this plan will work. It's also a great way to re-energize a store manager who has been in the same location for several years. I challenge you to put it to the test – you'll like the results.

# The 90 Day Turn-a-round

A Snapshot:

- Day 1-30 Gaining information and evaluating
- Day 31-60 Retraining and interviewing
- Day 61-90 Raising the bar and accountability

Envision a five level interchange on a major highway. There are on and off ramps, clover leafs, and merging lanes. At the beginning of this process, you are looking down on what appears to be a mess. There are cars trying to get off or on, others are driving in circles, one may be broken down on the side of the road, or even worse, in the middle of the lane causing a huge delay. From your vantage point, you can see the beautiful new six lane highway that lays just a few miles ahead. Your challenge is to get everyone off this crazy section of the highway and enter the new one, the straight one, the one with clear signs, easy to navigate and is actually going somewhere.

New Manager vs. Tenured Manager: In the first 30 days, the new manager is gathering information about their new store and team. The tenured manager is evaluating his current business and team members. From Days 31 – 90, the new manager and a tenured manager merge together and have the same focus.

# First 30 Days for the New Manager:

The first month is all about asking questions, observing and investigating. Back to our highway example; you have to understand where everyone is, how they got there, where they want to go and why they are there in the first place.

Ask questions such as: *Why do we do it that way*? This will not only give you insight into the operations of the store but also who understands and follows the company policies and procedures.

Observe procedures by requesting associates to demonstrate how to do different functions, such as: *Walk me through closing procedures. Show me how we do returns.*

One on ones are a must! But these are not about you, the manager, they are about gaining information about your new staff. Here are some suggested questions:

- How long have you worked here?

- Why have you stayed?

- What brought you to this company in the first place?

- What is your favorite part of this job?

- If I can change one thing to make your job perfect, what would it be?

- What's the biggest struggle our store has?

- What one thing do we have to fix ASAP?

Listen carefully to the answers; you're going to learn a lot. As you spend time with each employee, you want to be looking for experience, skills, and dedication for the position. You'll also want to find your leaders. Who should be promoted? Who has management potential? Who do you want on your team?

These first 30 days are your time to watch and listen. Observe everyone and everything. If you walk in with all your own plans and agendas, you may be successful. You may also lose the entire team. You need to see all the tools in the toolbox before you choose which one is best for the job. If you only see the hammer and only use the hammer, you'll be able to tear things down, but you won't be able to fix what's broken. You need to see and know the entire tool box to be able to make any long term plans.

Begin collecting current applications; you will need them next month. If you find there aren't any for your location, reach out to other managers. Find out how your company goes about generating applications and make sure steps are taken to generate a current flow.

As the new manager, you have not only acquired a new staff but also a store full of merchandise. The physical condition of the store is the condition of the road of this crazy five level interchange you are on. It's the potholes, the section that is always 'under construction'; it stands in the way of getting to that beautiful new six lane highway just a head. You can't fix everything at once – choose your battles carefully.

Start at the front door and work your way back. Go out the front door, turn around and enter the store. What is the first thing your customer sees when they walk in your door? Fix that and maintain it. The second priority is to fix the area around the register. If you enhance the first and last part of your customer's experience, the rest will be a blur to them. You will get to the Backroom on day 91 – it is part of the plan.

I love the analogy that when someone is hemorrhaging they shouldn't take the time to call the plastic surgeon in hopes of having their nose done. They have to stop the hemorrhaging. New manager – if you have taken over a new store that's in trouble, you have to stop the hemorrhaging and stabilize the business before you can make it beautiful. Get to know your people and how they operate. Begin to understand who will help you turn the store around. The plastic surgery comes later.

# First 30 Days for the Tenured Manager:

The first month is all about evaluating – *evaluating without excuses.* What are we evaluating?

Sales, Procedure, Backroom and most importantly, Staff.

Remember, there is no room for excuses now. You are obtaining the facts.

Do some role-play. Pretend you are a manager from another store. After spending a day in this store, how would you evaluate it?

Pretend you are the District Manager for this location. What is your evaluation of sales, staff and operations? Looking at your store through someone else's eyes gives you a new perspective.

Don't compare your store to someone else's unless it is a way to set a standard you want to achieve. Comparing your store to another store that is performing equal or less than yours only gives you more excuses for not making changes. It's only prestigious to be king of the best. Being king of mediocrity offers no crown.

# Sales

- What is the current trend?

- How far away are you from goal?

- What factors are preventing you from hitting the target?

- Why are sales down?

- Have you lost customers? If so, why?

- Are you profitable? What will it take to be profitable?

# Procedures

- Is the staff following policies and procedures or have they become lax?

- Has following policies and procedures taken priority over excellent customer service?

- What is taking up everyone's time?

- Are tasks evenly delegated or is one or two people doing the work?

- How is the tardiness track record? Who's coming in late on a regular basis?

# Backroom

Now that you know the secrets of the backroom, what does your Backroom say about you as a manger, your staff and your store's efficiency?

# Staff

- Who is making a difference in your store?

- Who is capable of turning the store around?

- Who has lost their drive?

- Who is burned out?

- Who is ready for the challenge?

If a fellow manager were to take over your store for one week, what would they say about your team?

If you had to be out and your district manager had to cover your shifts, what would they say about your team members?

You will need to collect applications so you are ready to interview next month. This may requires a sign in the window, ad on Craig's List or contacting your HR. Assuring you have a current application flow is essential.

This is no easy task for any tenured manager. It is important that a District Manager or fellow manager is part of the process to offer an extra point of view. If a manager could see what needs to be fixed, they would fix it. A tenured manager, who is experiencing a negative trend and has not taken steps to fix it, has lost the ability to see the situation clearly; an extra set of eyes is required.

## DAY 31 – 60

By this time, both the new manager and the tenured manager have all the information they need. The second month focuses on revisiting company policies and procedures and reading specific training material relating to the greatest needs of the store.

Example: if you are noticing a tardiness issue, pull out the policy on time and attendance and have everyone read and sign a copy. Now everyone understands and is starting at the same point.

Start with policies that affect everyday tasks. It really doesn't matter if everyone knows how to sell a gift card if you only sell five gift cards a year. On the other hand, if you sell five a day, everyone should know how to do it. This is a great time to use your strong players. You have a lot to do, so delegate this task. Go over the policy with one or two leaders within the team, making sure they understand the policy. Now give them the task of training others. By doing this, you will not only get everyone trained, but you will begin to identify who can follow through with your instructions and who has strong training skills.

This month is your foundation building month. Last month

you found all the cracks, this month you begin repairing. The first step in repairing is to make sure everyone is on the same page and the directions are clear. Your company's policy and procedures guide needs to be used daily. If you have to retrain everyone, make sure they are learning the right way the first time.

# Interviewing

Interviewing is also a key element! Both managers need to interview at least two applicants each week during the second month. A new manager will most likely need to hire. The tenured manager needs to see what talent is available. Something very interesting happens to a staff when they realize their manager is interviewing new talent. It sends a very strong and important message. For both staffs, the message is loud and clear: we have to change!

The new and the tenured manager need to spend time learning and/or revisiting their company's training on providing feedback, having honest conversations, documentation and holding the team accountable. These are all essential skills that will make month three greatly successful.

As far as the sales floor, choose five of the easiest fixes from your undoubtedly long list of "things that need attention". The second month is about staff development and training. Do not get focused on dusting the corners of the store, they have been in need of dusting for a long time, 30 more days isn't going to make that big of a difference.

## DAY 60 – 90

This final phase focuses on training new staff and holding current staff accountable. Both teams have been given 60 days to adjust. They have been given time to express their concerns. They have all the tools they need to do the job right – it's time to hold them accountable. Fear not, for those managers that struggle with accountability, by this time you will have pages filled with notes, observations and signed policies. Giving honest feedback now will be as simple as reading through your notes.

Back to the interchange example, month three is where you assist your team in finding the new highway or exiting safely. Once your team hits that new highway, they have to be ready and equipped to soar. You have fixed the road, repaired the vehicles and given clear directions. What you cannot control is the course the driver (your associate) chooses to take. What you can control is your level of commitment to staying on course and finishing well. What is so exiting about this 90 day adventure is that the end is just the beginning.

## 91 Days and Beyond!

Most managers seem to get stuck somewhere between the final exit on the interchange and the highway. They find themselves 6 months down the road asking why they continue to deal with the same issues. It takes determination to get on the new highway. On day 91, take time to stop and re-evaluate.

- How far have you come?

- What successes have you seen?

- Who is the diamond in the rough that is now sparkling?

- What are your customers saying?

- What are your sales saying?


*Most importantly –*

*Where is this new highway going to take you?*

# Part 2
# People

# People

When asked, "Who was your favorite boss?" One person comes to mind. He was the guy that after my second interview, I told my husband, "I'm not sure about this company, but I would love a chance to work for that guy!" There aren't too many of those around.

That guy had some great quotes. Most made me roll my eyes but every one of them made me laugh. One of my all time favorites was, "This job would be so easy if it weren't for f\*\*ken' people." When you are in the service industry; retail, foodservice, hospitality, everything you do is about people. They are the X factor in every equation. We can make budget plans, hiring goals, sales contests, but nothing can work without people. People need to serve and people need to be served.

Managing people is most likely the toughest part of any management position. From hiring to training to promoting to terminating, it is a complicated and difficult task. In this section, we are going to only touch on the topic of People. Undoubtedly your company has policies on managing people. In addition, there are volumes written on the subject and volumes are still forthcoming.

"This job would be so easy if it weren't for f**ken' people!"

# Staffing

Knowing when to staff and how many to staff is an art. There was a time when payroll wasn't tight and companies could afford extra staff. Post 2008, there are no extras allowed. Shifts that once offered 6 people hours are now done with 3 or possibly 4 if you are lucky. However, being overstaffed is just as difficult as being understaffed. Staffing needs are based on the flux in business; it is ever changing and so are your staffing needs.

The first rule is to never think that you are done! Staffing is a revolving door; managers can only manage the door. The better you manage how fast that door revolves, the easier it is to plan. Over the years, I have watched managers struggle with staffing issues. I quickly realized that just as there are similarities in Management Styles, there are similarities in how managers approach staffing.

# Staffing Styles –

## Group 1

This manager always plans ahead. Typically they have more staff than hours available for scheduling. They rarely find themselves shorthanded and are likely to be the store that can afford to share staff.

The staff at these stores understands that hours are earned not promised. Those that contribute the most receive the most hours. They also understand that if they fail to contribute, there is someone available to take their place. These managers will always build a team, not a staff. This team holds themselves and each other accountable to the manager's high standards. This accountability is out of respect for the position and manager not out of fear of screwing up.

This manager is never without a constant flow of applications. Great people want to work in great environments; such environments can be observed by the outsider.

Because of this solid staffing style, these managers always seem relaxed and in control. They have the time and desire to take on additional work. Although losing a team member is difficult, these managers have someone waiting in the wings to move in. Managing the revolving door is easy because this manager knows his team and the team trusts him. Communication flows freely between he and his team and rarely is he caught off guard.

It is in the numbers where one can truly judge the strength of a manager and his team. This manager has the ability to post positive year on year increases. He executes company promotions and directives effortlessly. This is the store that seems to find the time to get involved in their community. The team exemplifies the company's culture in everything they do. The store's operations are always 90 to 100% accurate. This team usually exceeds the company averages and goals. The atmosphere in the store is positive, energized and contagious.

Because this manager understands the importance of staffing and building a team, he is the manager that rarely burns out.

## Group 2

This manager has enough staff to write a schedule. There is always sufficient key holders or supervisors. However, she has an underlying fear that someone may quit, leaving her shorthanded.

Although policy and procedures are followed, she allows things to slide not because she doesn't think they are important, but because she is afraid that if she pushes too hard and would have to actually terminate someone, she will be left working the extra hours. As a result, the staff becomes sloppy, taking short cuts, and possibly showing an increasing lack of respect for their manager.

An interesting phenomenon begins when a staff knows there is little to no extra schedule coverage available within the current staff, requests off happen more frequently. This comes when the realization hits them that there isn't anyone who could take their place, in other words, they aren't replaceable.

Finding new staff members is increasingly difficult because the application flow is mixed. When staffing is an issue, the manager is stressed more than usual. Company directives lag in their execution and the overall energy of the store is lacking. Great applicants will sense this immediately and will be reluctant to apply.

Overall this is a good team, but it's not great. This manager and store operates somewhere between 80 – 90% of their potential. Staffing stress wears a manager down faster than any other stress. This manager lasts two to three years before they burn out.

# Group 3

This manager has just enough staff. If everyone works what they said they could, they can actually write a schedule. If someone goes on vacation or God forbid calls in sick, there is no one to cover. The manager lives in constant fear that someone will quit. And if available, this store is continually calling other stores in the area to get shifts covered.

When a store becomes understaffed, even the slightest bit, the manager is unable to hold anyone accountable due to the lack of back up. Once the balance of accountability begins to shift, a manager quickly begins to lose control. Late arrivals, no shows, calling in sick at the last minute, seem to happen on a regular basis. When a manager is spending most of his time finding people to cover shifts or even worse, having to cover them himself, there is little time for anything else. This shift in staffing quickly creates a shift in authority. The old saying that the inmates are controlling the asylum describes this store's culture to the T. This may sound harsh, but if teams, staffs, employees did what they were supposed to do all the time, there would be no need for managers. The position of manager was created because teams, staffs and employees don't always do what they are supposed to, thus they need to be managed, thus we need managers. When a staff becomes the manager and the manager becomes the one doing everything, the world is upside down and it doesn't work well that way.

A manager who finds himself in this situation will also find it difficult to find new team members. If this manager is going to turn this around, he will need to go out and find applicants either by recruiting or asking other store managers, whose stores are running well, to pass off any great apps they are unable to use.

As for the condition of these stores and managers, they are

both stressed. Operations are running at about 60 -75% of where they should run. Deadlines are not met, directives are not followed. The manager lives in fear that one more person may quit and is exhausted from being the one man show. Any good employees quickly become resentful because of the work load they are being asked to pickup, not to make the workplace better but because someone else isn't doing their job. These stores will typically begin running in negative comps and most likely have an increase in customer complaints. These managers will last less than a year in the current condition.

# Group 4

This manager has become a full-time employee instead of the manager. She is forced to work an enormous amount of hours on the floor filling shifts. She no longer is afraid someone will leave, she pleads for people to stay. She has lost control of her store and her team.

The staff has little to no respect for their manager. There are daily phone calls from team members who are not asking for time off, rather informing the manager they are not coming in today. There is no application flow and if there were, the manager doesn't have time to interview. Rather, the current staff is recommending their friends as possible applicants. Bad employees will recommend bad employees. In many cases these teams resemble a frat house rather than a staff.

The operations of this store are falling quickly. Sales goals, directives and passed deadlines pile up on the manager's desk – which is mostly a mess.

As if overnight, this store will become dirty and unkept. Customer service is nowhere to be found and the overworked, overstressed manager has a growing anger and resentment towards her team and the company. If they last six months, it's amazing as this manager will burn out quickly.

Staffing issues can turn bad quickly, especially in a small staff. If a manager only has five to six staff members, it only takes one to leave unexpectedly to start the downward spiral. Great managers are always prepared for the unexpected. A great manager also knows that when staffing becomes an issue, everything else stops until staffing is back on track. Without great teams, there are no great managers.

# Hiring

We currently live in a world where all our hiring decisions are made on the computer. Unless you are hiring someone to fill out applications all day long on a computer, the computer should not be the one making the decision who is best for the job. A computer cannot show personality. It is incapable of judging a prospective employee's ability to sell.

The company I was with, when on-line hiring started to be the new way of staffing, wanted to set up the profile they would use for all future applicants by bringing in the most successful managers to answer a lengthy questionnaire. These answers would become the bench mark for future hires. It sounds good in theory. However, many of these people had been with the company two, five even ten years. The bench mark was set at a level of who they had become, not who they were when they were hired. If each one were to apply for the same position now based on the new query, it is likely that none of them would have ever been hired.

Hiring has to happen with personal contact. This is where first impressions do matter. If an applicant doesn't care enough to look different for an interview than they would go to the beach, it is likely that they will act as if they are at the beach when they are working. Employees have to take pride in their work and pride in themselves, their appearance reflects that level of pride. Judging one's appearance is not judging who they are but how important this job is to them. Appearance here does not refer to their looks. It refers to their style, smile, eye contact, and their ability to interact.

If you work for a company that does all on-line application, use this system as only part of the process. When someone walks into your store inquiring about a job and they appear to be exactly what you are looking for, STOP WHAT YOU ARE DOING AND TALK TO THEM!!! After a short conversation, tell them to go on-line and fill out the application. Once complete, you'll give them a call and set up an interview. Then wait for that application. It's the first test in how well they follow through and how much they really want this job.

Be creative with your interviewing and listen well. Walk around the store with them. Ask them questions about the store; the layout, the cleanliness, what looks like it needs attention. Some of the best interviews I've done turned out to be the people who, after they were hired, had no idea how to work, they spoke well, but actually working was foreign. The best hires I have made were people that when we walked through the store, pointed out things that needed to be changed, corners that needed to be cleaned and customer service issues they were observing. Before they ever filled out the I-9s, they were ready to go. If you aren't experienced with interviewing, do it even if you don't need to hire. Do it for the experience. Who's to say someone may just surprise you, and you find what you need before you need it.

I will confess that the absolute best hires I have made happened in a very non-business manner. They were on days that as I was getting ready for work, I was thinking of the type of person I needed to find, the skills that they needed to bring with them and the experience that would enhance the business. On the way to work, I imagined what it would be like to have them part of the team, how my workload would shift and the difference they would make. As I unlocked the front door of the store I simply said, "God, I need one of them." It is later that afternoon when *one of them* walked through those same front doors, application in hand, smile on their face and hand held out to be greeted that I chuckle to myself and say, "Why can't it happen like this all the time?"

It doesn't matter how long you've done this job or how many hires you've made, no one hires perfectly all the time. There are those who interview well and suck at the job. There are those who nervously interact with you during the interview and once they are behind the counter, turn into superman. The skill of interviewing and hiring improves over time, but it is never perfect. We will all misread someone – this is why most companies have a 90 days probation period. It allows us to fix our mistakes quickly.

# When to Hire

There are definitely hiring trends in business. One company freezes all new hires from May 1st through July 15th. Why would they do such a thing? Because they have found that the majority of new hires who have come into their company during this time are more likely to leave by the end of the year, if not by the end of summer. By setting the perimeter, they have managed their turnover as well as forced their managers to plan ahead.

Knowing when to hire, especially when you have a small staff can be very challenging. If you are running with a skeleton crew, it's just as difficult having too many people than too few. When you are overstaffed, everyone is crying for more hours.

When you are understaffed, people can become overworked.

Hands down, I would choose to be overstaffed anytime. There is a laxness that can come when a store is understaffed. It comes from the concept; *I no longer need this job more than this job needs me. I can be late, I can be a little lazy, after all, they aren't going to fire me! Who would work?*

A team should realize that hours are earned, especially in a small staff. A manager needs every person to be pulling their own weight; they can't afford to give hours away to those who are not productive.

Take time to look ahead. It could take time to find a great person and you never – ever want to be in the position that you have to hire because you NEED someone. First, you want to look at your business. When are your peak seasons? Are you expecting a jump in sales? If you had one more person, would you be able to push your sales higher? Can you squeeze in one more person during your busiest time to make sales even more profitable?

Next, you need to evaluate your current staff. Who is possibly going to have a life change and leave you? Who is underperforming? Are they going to be able to turn things around or when you start holding them accountable, will they bail on you?

It never hurts to interview even if you aren't hiring. Interviewing when there doesn't seem to be a present need allows you to see what the talent pool looks like. Sometimes it's better to work with what you have than gambling on someone new. Sometimes you may find the gem you've been waiting for all your life and you'll find a way to fit them in.

The attitude is, "I'm always looking for great people!" The reality is that you are not always in control of when those great people will show up. So be watching for them.

# Building a Team

Building a team and team building are two different things. Team building is done once a team is in place with the goal of creating a stronger bond between the individual members of the team. Building a team is the beginning point; it is when you are selecting players for your team.

Most managers inherit a team. However, if you are fortunate enough to be building a team from scratch, you have the benefit of choosing who you want. The downside here is when someone doesn't work out, and there will be at least one, you don't have the 'other' manager to blame, they all belong to you! The upside to inheriting a team is you have the opportunity to observe their behaviors and skill set prior to deciding if they will make the cut.

So, what do you look for when building a team? Many managers simply look at availability; never, never, ever hire someone based strictly on their availability, availabilities change. Poor managers hire based on schedule, strong managers hire based on the needs of their business.

The other hire that you want to avoid is hiring friends of your current employees. It is rare to find a friend who needs a job that is actually a hard worker. A team made up of friends is a party, not a staff.

Diversity in a team is essential. You should be looking for people with different skill sets than yours. It never hurts to have a few people around that are smarter then you. Diversity comes when teams have different interests, different skill sets, varies in age, in size, shape and color.

Why is diversity important? Something unique happens when a group of people who are not all alike come together for one purpose. A new level of creativity is created. Ideas are as diverse as those offering them. Problem solving becomes much easier with so many to draw from. There seems to be less negative competition between the team members as they learn to accept the difference each one brings to the group. Less important, but still a great benefit, is the guarantee that the chit-chat that happens through the course of the day is far more entertaining with a diverse team. Finally, customers respond far better to a diverse team as they are more likely to find someone with whom they can relate.

When building a team, there is nothing wrong with recruiting people you have worked with in the past. If you choose this route, understand that taking an employee from another employer will most likely happen to you someday. So no bitching down the road when your best team member hands in their resignation because the guy across the street has wooed them over. It's that old 'do unto other's' thing that seems to be more of a fact of life than just a nice proverb. If you feel it is an appropriate way for you to obtain your team, then you need to respect other managers who do the same.

Be very careful not to hire personal friends. There are very few friendships than can handle one of the friends becoming the boss. No matter how strong a friendship is, few rarely survive working together.

Building teams can be one of the most enjoyable parts of management. Compare it to baking a pie. It's not a pie if all you have is crust. No matter how much crust you have, it doesn't work. You need all the diverse ingredients - combined together to create an amazing aroma and mouthwatering taste. A pile of apples on a plate a pie does not make. Sugar and cinnamon, butter and crunch all blended together produces something that no one can resist.

Once this diverse team is created, you, as the manager, must always remember YOU ARE THE LEADER. Keep your relationship professional. This amazing team that you have brought together can easily draw you into their lives and activities; resist the temptation. When asked to join them for drinks – step carefully. Once you show up to a party attended by your employees, the party quickly becomes a business activity in the eyes of the law. Don't take chances. You worked hard to build this team, protect your relationship with them. Don't do something stupid to ruin it. This is in no way saying not to find ways to interact and build relationships. It is to say that when you find opportunities to build stronger and deeper relationships with your team, that you keep it on a very professional basis. They deserve it and you've worked much too hard to find yourself in a position of cleaning up a mess and starting all over.

# Training

A well trained staff typically is also a long tenured staff. People like to be experts. Employees like to know how things work, why procedures are in place and most of all, how to move forward in a company. An employee should always be in training. From day one, learning how to clock in, to year five, continual learning keeps us all motivated.

The first place to start is with your company's training material. Whether this material is the best training program you've ever seen or if it leaves a lot to be desired, it's the beginning. Once you and your team are experts, you can begin creating additional material.

When you think of all the things to be taught and learned

within your company and field, training never stops. The first focus needs to be on policy and procedures. Be creative in your training. Don't throw a manual at someone and tell them to learn it. Pull it apart. Make it a group experience. Everyone can benefit from reviewing policy and procedures. For your newest employee, challenge him to read the policy and then watch to see if the current team is following it. If not, it's time to retrain. We all get sloppy, we all take a short cut from time to time. New employees are a great way to ensure that you are never losing sight of the basics.

Next is product knowledge. We can never know too much about the product we sell. We can, however, overwhelm our customers with the extent of our knowledge. Product knowledge allows employees to speak intelligently to the customer. When it comes to successful selling, product knowledge is a key component.

Whether you are selling food, services, hard or soft lines, knowing where your product comes from, how it works, what care is needed to maintain it, as well as it's uses, grants the sales person a level of expertise that will not only allow him to sell more, but if communicated correctly, builds a level of trust with the customer.

The simple guideline for product knowledge training is:

• What is the product?

• Where did it come from?

- How does it work?

- What care is required?

- If it is an agriculture item; How does it grow?


A team that is well trained demonstrates a level of confidence and commitment to the job. The old adage, "Knowledge is Power" holds very true when it comes to developing employees as well as successful selling skills.

Business and financial training follows product knowledge. Not everyone enjoys reading a Profit and Loss statement. Those who do should have the privilege of doing so. Training members of your team to control line items on your budget, such as payroll, supplies and inventory, furthers their understanding of running a business. It also gives you support when budgets are cut or adjustments have to be made. A team that understands the balance between sales and scheduling understands the impact of loss of sales. It also will move some employees into positions of leadership. There's great advantages to having team members who understand business and financials, even if it's at a beginner's level.

In the early 90's, a company named Caribou Coffee had a core value that stated, "Each one teach one." It's a great value. If each one of your team members taught just one other team member one thing every shift, your job would suddenly become much easier. Every time you show someone a new procedure or correct a practice, tell them to train one other person. This simple act has great benefits. It will solidify what you have just taught. It tells your employee that you have confidence in him to train someone else. In training another person, the employee is now practicing what they have learned, they will not forget again. Once this concept of training each other takes hold, your struggle to get everyone on the same page will end.

# Development

I believe there is a world of difference between Training and Development. Training tells me what tasks are expected. Development teaches me how to do them. Anyone can read a policy book or training manual. How one follows those policies and procedures is based on their development.

Development requires an investment in time and money. It is becoming increasingly rare for companies to spend the time needed to develop their managers. The outcome is a team of managers who can repeat the rules but lack the ability to run a business. A company's level of respect for the manager's position is directly related to the time invested in their development.

The same goes for a manager. A manager's level of respect for his team is directly related to the time invested in developing individuals. A *training manager* will tell his new hires that providing excellent customer service is part of the job requirement. The *developer manager* will spend time explaining and demonstrating what excellent customer service looks like.

Being a part of someone's development requires a lot of observing. In those observations, the challenge is to pinpoint their strengths and then begin to build on them. If you have a trainer on your team, work with him/her; give him/her every opportunity to improve their skill by training others. For that person who is always asking for clarification on reports, let them be a part of your weekly business review. Spend time explaining what and how the percentages are figured. What do they mean and how does it affect your business. Then get them involved in setting sales goals, or creating a plan that focuses on one line item that needs attention.

Development takes time and patience. A manager who takes the time to develop those on her team will find herself with less and less to do, as her team members become more and more responsible and invested in the business. For the team members, they will be learning skills that can be used elsewhere. However, team members who work under a manager who is willing to invest time in their development become very loyal and unless an opportunity finds them, they rarely go looking for one. They like where they work.

# Managing People

The most complicated part of this people piece is dealing with issues, addressing poor behavior and confronting people. It is the most complicated and the most rewarding. It takes time to master the skills needed but once mastered, the art of dealing with people will only allow you to be more successful than you are currently. We are moving out of hiring and training into people management.

# Write It Down

Did you document it? Documentation does not have to be complicated. Parents are forever telling kids, "If you put it away after you used it, you would never have a mess!" It's the same for managers, "If you document it when it happens, you'll never have a mess." There is nothing worse than having an employee who is making your life hell and you can't do anything about it because you didn't document it from the beginning. Documentation takes discipline and consistent documentation divides the weak from the strong.

Documentation is simple: "Fred was late on Sunday 2/1, Friday 2/5 and Saturday 2/6".

The conversation can also be simple, "Fred, I want you to know that I write everything down. I want everyone to know what is in their personnel files, so here is a note stating that you were late three times this week. I would like for you to sign it stating that you saw it – it doesn't mean you agree – but you don't have to sign it, it's going in your file either way."

Fred will look a bit shocked. He may or may not sign the paper.

"You need to fix this tardiness issue, Fred. If you don't, it could affect your ability to work here."

In a two minute conversation, Fred is aware that he has an issue, that you are not going to let it get out of control and that he needs to correct it. Fred's level of respect for you as his manager has just increased and you have taken control of the situation quickly and respectfully. You have done your part, the rest is up to Fred. If Fred doesn't sign the paper, don't let it stop you from putting it in Fred's file. In those situations, attach a simple note: on 2/10 Discussed tardiness issues with Fred. Fred did not sign the document.

Most HR departments have a variety of forms that can be used for documentation. Don't let your intimidation of the forms stop you from documenting. A handwritten piece of paper can always be stapled to a form. If you're unfamiliar with your company's forms, shame on them for not taking the time to train you of their use, but that can't stop you. Take time to learn how to use them and then use them.

In our current world, it seems to take a lot of documentation to terminate someone. Stay ahead of the issue. A piece of notebook paper with your notes on it is better than only memories in your head. No one is ever terminated because their manager remembered something.

Documentation is not only for the wrong. If you document the good and the bad, you will appear very balanced and fair to your team. How often do we hear someone say, "He only sees the bad." Even if it's not the case, commenting and documenting only the bad makes it appear this way.

# Honest Not Tough

Why do we become so emotionally involved that we are unable to have honest, straightforward conversations with those who work for us?  There are a multitude of reasons:

"I don't want to be the bad guy."

"What will I look like?"

"But they are so nice, I don't want them to feel bad."

We have built a mentality around giving feedback that has become so intimidating even the strongest manager has moments of butterflies before such discussions.  There are outlines, fill in the blank forms, even books on giving feedback.

We refer to it as "tough conversations" - a term that does little to calm the nerves. We have created mountains out of what should simply be honest conversations.

In order for an honest conversation to be meaningful and impactful, it must be delivered with integrity, honesty and presented in a very transparent way. The receiver needs to believe that they are important and what is being discussed is a behavior not a personality trait. Behaviors are teachable; personality traits take much longer to mold and are not the responsibility of an employer.

The key to creating an honest work environment where such conversations are not only expected but desired is to simply have *continual meaningful conversations*. One-on-ones that have purpose; making sure that performance related conversations are happening around good and not so good behaviors. If the only time my boss sits down with me is to point out what I need to improve on, I will become defensive. Again we hear, *they only point out what's wrong, doesn't anyone see when I do it right?*

One-on-ones need to be two-way conversations. There is a wealth of ideas, reasons and even excuses employees need to be able to communicate. Your team is your front line; their experiences and input is essential for you to understand what is transpiring outside of your peripheral vision. What may seem as someone's inability to complete a task properly may be due to how they were trained. For the employees, they are doing what they believe is right and you are assuming they are being defiant.

One-on-ones with purpose can be motivating for both parties. It is a time to build a professional relationship, talk about future goals, set clear expectations and learn from each other.

There are a few guidelines to keep in mind:

It is important to get to know our employees but be careful not to use your understanding of their personal life as an excuse for poor performance.

Keep this time business focused. It is easy to waste this time. Both parties need to walk away with a game plan.

- What needs to be improved upon?

- What issues need to be looked into?

- What company policy and procedures need to be improved in order to be more successful?

- What's getting in the way of becoming excellent at our job?

- What strengths need to be leveraged?

- What strengths need to be further developed?

- What seems to be a roadblock that we need to work around?

When an employee walks away from this type of conversation, they know they have been heard. It opens the door for further

conversations. It establishes a professional relationship built on trust and respect. Both parties also begin to understand there are roadblocks that are unmovable and we have to be smart enough to work together to figure out how to use them to our advantage.

When a manager develops a core of people that are free to have open and honest communication with each other, it becomes contagious. Individuals begin to look within themselves and become more and more comfortable asking for help to develop their own weaknesses. This type of work environment will create a core of employees who become very protective of this new culture and will not allow anyone or anything to get in its way. For the manager, they become the dream team.

# Let's Talk Standards
# for a Minute...

I believe punctuality and the ability to follow dress code tells a lot about employees. These are the two areas that managers have no control. The ability to arrive to work on time and in uniform is 100% the employee's responsibility. My conversation went just like this, "I don't dress you or pick you up for work, that's your job. Your commitment to do those two things shows me your ability and commitment to the job." I guarantee that an employee who doesn't feel the need to follow dress code or arrive to work on time, is likely not following other rules as well. It seems silly to be fired because one can't get to work on time, but time management, commitment to co-workers, respect for the company and manager are all rolled up into that one task.

Documenting tardiness is simple because of time cards. Dress code issues take a disciplined manager to document and discuss those issues with the employee.

Signed copies of policies and procedures are helpful in supporting documentation. It never hurts to pull out the dress code policy for the struggling employee, have them read and sign it and place it in their file. This will also prove to them that you aren't playing games. It will also come in handy if they decide they are above such policies and decide not to follow them.

What you have to remember when documenting and disciplining is that if you are going to document one employee for tardiness, you must document all. If punctuality hasn't been a focus and suddenly you realize you have an issue, don't look at just one person's time card. Look at the entire team's – including yours! Sam can't be disciplined for something that Fred, Sally, Tom and Betty are also doing. If you find that you have a group issue, pull out the policy, and have everyone sign it. This puts everyone on an equal playing field. It also gives you a fresh start. You may find out that Sam really doesn't have a time issue but rather, he has no respect for Fred, his supervisor, because Fred is always late.

Responsibility and trust come to those who prove they can handle the simple things; tardiness and dress code are about as simple as it gets.

# Then There are Projects!

We refer to them as projects. They are the employees who seem to take most of your time and energy. There is something deep within us that says, "They can do this job." They can cause conflict among other staff members. Some will stick with it and become shining stars, others will simply suck the life out of you.

When it comes to these projects, managers need to walk carefully and ask themselves a few questions:

- Do I have time for this?

- What is the negative effects on the team and business while this person is figuring out the job.

- How much am I willing to sacrifice for them?

If you are a new manager or recently taken over a new position, you don't have time for projects. If you are a struggling manager, you need to be surrounding yourself with bright, talented people. You are the project and all your time and energy needs to go into you.

I have had projects that have been well worth every ounce of time and energy I poured into them. And I have had projects that were a great disappointment and cost me much more than time and energy.

## This is one of my many projects...

You know the type, thirty-something with attitude. Always seems to be out to prove something. No one ever does it right or at least could ever do it as well as they could. They anger those who are unable to speak out for themselves and frustrate those who have a crushed self-image. They cause drama and stress and can rip apart a team faster than they can be terminated.

Sadly, there is an endless supply of this individual and management is where they like to be. It gives them power to control, to force their opinion because, they have been handed a title that says it is all right for them to do so. Management is empowering to them.

Typically, they job hop, either they leave because they hit

too many brick walls or boredom sets in because in reality, they are not open to learning new ways of management or experimenting with new concepts. They do it the same way in every job and why should they change? They believe they are always right. After all, they are the experts, it is their way and if you do not like it, they are not here to make friends. They are here to do a job.

Rhonda was five weeks into her training. She had interviewed very well, passed all the tests. I made her an offer and set up a time for her orientation. During orientation, a few comments were said that made me wonder if I had made a mistake. Rhonda was placed with a very seasoned manager with a very strong personality. In the first three weeks, she flew through her training modules, always making sure that I was informed of her amazing progress and determination to be great. The team at this particular training store tried their best to accept her and make her feel welcome. By her third week of training, they had decided they really did not like her and wanted her to finish training and move on.

Her training manager raved about her for the first three weeks. She was excelling in her training. She knew the answer before the question was even asked. She came to work prepared. She was always ahead in her reading. *I have no doubt she will be very successful*, was the response I received on a regular basis.

Then week four hit. Schedule changes, daily drama and a team of peers that were quickly building walls. It is amazing how someone can be impressive in the first 21 days and by day 22, the honeymoon is over and the real person emerges. I had dealt with this before and was not sure I wanted to take on a project that I knew had no guarantee of a positive outcome. I needed to do something quickly.

In the position I was in, I spent a lot of time on the road. This in no way was exciting travel. It was getting in the car and making two to three hour road trips along the most boring roadways in America. A lot of time on the road translates into a lot of time to think. One can only eat, make phone calls and try to read emails on the Blackberry for so long when one is driving hours alone. I had actually become very accomplished at eating a taco salad from Wendy's, talking on the phone and driving with my knee; that was back when it was legal to do so.

During my three hour drive, I had plenty of time to prepare my speech. From past experience, I knew I did not want to have this issue creep into my team. They were a great team and I had worked very hard to create that environment. I also knew that this management style would not be successful in my stores. If change did not happen and I allowed her to take over one of my stores, I would be replacing her within a year and most likely have to re-staff the store several times. So the verdict was in, Rhonda needed to go.

I had learned to deliver a very quick termination; the two minute termination had been part of my development. By the time you have made the decision to terminate someone, the discussion time is over. Leading up to a termination it is essential that you lay a very clear set of expectations that allow you to hold someone accountable to the Nth degree. I had already decided that this was not going to work and I needed to remove Rhonda quickly.

I already had a meeting set up so there was no need to schedule one. The trip there gave me three hours to prepare. Halfway there I felt I was ready.

- You are a very strong individual
- You bring a lot of experience to the table
- Tell me about your conversations with Manager A and Manager B.
- How are you getting along with the team at your training store?
- You are coming across too harsh and you need to change

Some conversation between points and the groundwork would be laid for future conversations as needed. I was confident.

A few miles later, I was reminded of the bosses that had dealt with me so strongly. I was a young manager with a ton of drive and ideas and not a lot of training on how to communicate those ideas, so I put a lot of people at arms length. Who would

I be today if someone would have come alongside of me and taught me how to communicate rather than dodging the 2x4s aimed at the side of my head? I had been broken many times and found myself for years afraid to offer any opinion and second guessing myself, which in turn made me ever more ineffective.

I had recalled during our interview that the statement was made, "I'm not afraid to work, my friends call me a workaholic". Interesting description of oneself, I had thought at the time. Most people deny this title or make excuses; this one claimed it and in some odd way was proud of it.

We did not have a lot of time scheduled so I knew I needed to stay on task. However, I did arrange the day so the last person I sat down with was Rhonda. Not knowing what the response would be, I wanted to make sure I did have time to talk and not rush off to another meeting.

Our conversation began with the basics; how is your training going? Are there any areas you feel you want to spend more time on before training ends? I expressed that I had no doubt that she could do the job, she was smart, she had plenty of experience and she was doing well with training but I had a few questions. I repeated her statement claiming to be a workaholic and simply asked why had she chosen to live that way? I had hit the nerve, pulled the plug out of the dike in just a few minutes.

The remainder of our conversation lasted about 40 minutes

and it was full of emotion. This tough, opinionated, confident woman had in a few short minutes opened up and I now had a very clear picture of what I was dealing with. She became very vulnerable sharing past experiences, fears and lack of self- confidence.

The next day was quite amusing. It is not fair to say it was like watching a bull in a china shop. This was much more like watching a bull in a Toto trying to dance in a china shop. Obviously, this was going to take some time and even more obvious was the fact that she was going to need a lot of coaching. What had started out to be a conversation to set the groundwork for termination, had turned into a conversations which laid the ground work for several more conversation and opportunities to coach someone who had decided to use her drive to improve her own management style.

It is a very fine balance between coaching/developing and becoming a personal counselor. Business has to be business and there is some truth in the statement that we are not here to make friends, we are here to do a job. However, when one can create an environment where individuals can safely discuss their weaknesses and honest conversations can happen to motivate and challenge each other to become better, the balance will remain and people will grow.

Rhonda tried to play a few manipulative games during the next week. It lasted a very short time. Rhonda is very smart and it did not take her long to realize that no one was buying the "woe is me" routine.

I do have a quick fix for those *woe is me* conversations. I like to refer to it as the "My life sucks more than yours" Award. This is a great recognition to give when you have someone that is unable to stop complaining about how much he or she has going on or how his or her life is so tough. I give this out on a regular basis; it can quickly turn a negative conversation into laughter and acknowledgment that you understand their current frustration level. Everyone wants to be recognized for something.

Rhonda quickly got the message that I was willing to work with her but that I was expecting her to soften her style and build relationships with her team and her peers and that does not happen when you talk loudly and carry a big stick. She still struggles with the tough image she projects but she is working hard to keep a balance.

Shortly after our conversation, Rhonda had to witness a termination. As she was telling me about it, she became very emotional. Tears filled her eyes as she admitted that she really had only terminated one person and she had to lock herself in the office and cry afterwards. Witnessing this termination was tearing her apart. I was bewildered. This tough, confident drill sergeant, who once was so quick to respond that she was not here to make friends; she was hired to do a job and if the team did not like it, there's the door, had only terminated one person in her entire career.

Tough exteriors are usually there to protect a very sensitive interior. This is true with both males and females. Those who bark loudly usually do not have any teeth in which to bite.

Where would I be today if someone had come alongside and showed me how to...

# Indifference

**Noun**

1: unbiased impartial unconcern

2: apathy demonstrated by an absence of emotional reactions [syn: emotionlessness, impassivity, impassiveness, phlegm, stolidity, unemotionality]

3: the trait of lacking enthusiasm for or interest in things generally [syn: apathy, spiritlessness]

4: the trait of remaining calm and seeming not to care; a casual lack of concern [syn: nonchalance, unconcern]

I would much rather be sitting at a table surrounded by a group of managers who are opinionated, passionate and emotional than teamed with one who is indifferent. What can one possibly do with an individual who is indifferent toward their job?

Granted there are some admirable characteristics in what defines *indifference*: *unbiased, impartial, absence of emotional reactions, the trait of remaining calm.* These character traits can show signs of maturity. Individuals that are not reactive usually make very sound judgment calls. Someone who is unbiased and impartial can build teams that are diverse. Someone who can make decisions that are unbiased or impartial is admired and sought after because they are not swayed by emotions.

The problem comes when these traits are paired up with *unconcern, the trait of lacking enthusiasm for or interest in things generally, seeming not to care.* When employees are being hired, trained and managed by an individual that lacks enthusiasm, or is unconcerned and seems not to care there will ultimately be a lack of standards, policy and overall loyalty to the company.

I've known many managers who were indifferent. They range in experience level, education, personalities and maturity. What they do have in common is they have become ineffective in the position. For most, if they are forced to think back to when they started feeling this way, they can go back to one experience.

Most will go back to a change in management, being passed over for a promotion, change in company focus; some may even take it back to a traumatic personal experience. Somewhere along the way, an event has transpired that is bigger than their ability to overcome and the result is, "I just don't care anymore".

# She Ain't Heavy - She's Just Sick

Opening a new store can be very exciting. No doubt there will be roadblocks. Product that does not ship, accounts that do not get set up, and contractors that use their own interpretation of blueprints and place fixtures in odd places. I have lost count of the number of stores I have been involved in opening. Each one is unique and each one brings its own challenges. Some have more roadblocks than others; some actually open on time.

This particular store was ready to go. The staff was hired and the manager was confident that this would be the best. The excitement built every day. The countdown had begun to opening day. The store looked great, the marketing department had out done themselves, and this was going to be a great opening.

I had worked a long time with this manager and her excitement and energy was contagious. I had left so many of the details to be handled by her, she was the most competent and confident manager I had. No doubts, no concerns. This one will be a home run, out of the ballpark. I was enjoying watching the process from a distance. It was rare that I did not have to be involved in every detail. Then, out of nowhere began the phone calls, Doctors appointments, test results, red blood cell counts, white blood cell counts, surgery, operations, recovery, treatments. Terms that were not part of the 90 day plan.

This person, the single most important part in the history of a new store, was beginning to crumble; emotions, tears, concerns, forgetfulness and fear. I needed to do what is best for her, making sure all the benefits were in place. FMLA, HIPA, leave of absence, daily conversations with the HR department, it can be exhausting. Not only was I focused on one person's needs but there was a team of people and business to take care of. There is no other time in management where compassion and concern walk hand-in-hand with control and decisiveness. It is a very emotional time.

Arrangements were made, coverage for six, eight possibly twelve weeks. I was half hoping and half expecting that she should be able to return in twelve weeks. I was assuming that there would be some follow-up treatment such as physical therapy and that we could handle. Twelve weeks can be a very long time. The store opened on time and for the first few weeks was running surprisingly smoothly. This was clearly a reflection of the quality of the team that my manager had brought together. The store was running fine but definitely not the same as if there was a manager present. Frequently I am reminded about how it could have been, should have been.

Finally, the doctor's release was given to return for administrative tasks only. Yes, at least she would have a presence back in her store and get reacquainted with the team she had hired and trained. It was in no way perfect but at least it was a start to getting things back to normal.

There was a new list of terms; medications, painkillers, hormones, mood swings, frustration, intolerance and more forgetfulness. I knew that somewhere in there was the person I hired, the one that I had watched handle all that pre-opening stress with laughter and excitement. Now I was never sure who would be on the other end of the phone, the person I knew or the person greatly affected by this life-changing event she had just walked through.

Another twelve weeks and she was three months back on the job. The store was doing fine. Several of the team had left and new hires were in place. All seemed to be returning to normal, but there were still moments. More doctors' visits, infections and changes in medication that caused mood swings and drained energy. Concern was building from above. Do we need to make a change? How long do we wait? Will she ever be back to normal?

It was easy to be confident early on. I was sure that this manager would be able to overcome, confident that she was worth the wait. Six months into it, my confidence was starting to waver. There were moments of normalcy. In the morning when I called the store, I would recognize the voice on the other end as that person I had hired. What a sense of relief that she was back, all was going to be fine. The next day, a frantic manager would be back on the phone unable to deal with the most minute incident. If I was seeing these extremes, what was the team seeing and how would it affect them?

Nine months had past and everything felt so much more stable. I was noticing some mood swings, definitely some forgetfulness. There were still times that the conversation would put me into a tailspin, wondering if I had not stepped into the Twilight Zone.

In the larger scheme of things, touring with my boss was an event that should have taken place quarterly. This is a time for him to spend with my managers, visiting stores and giving input. In the last year and a half, this had only happened once and it was forced. It is extremely important to have one-on-one time with one's boss. The lack of it can only result in miscommunication, misunderstandings and a great deal of confusion. Realizing this, I had taken the initiative to request that we schedule a day for touring a few of my stores. A date had been suggested but nothing had been confirmed.

On that particular morning, I had scheduled a business meeting with the above manager. I had not planned anything that would be too intense but, obviously, I had forgotten the superior role my boss enjoyed playing when store managers were the audience.

I spent the entire morning watching the front door to see if he would show. Sitting at a large table in front of the store, I was conducting our monthly business meeting. This is a time to go over last month's results and set goals for current month. I could not help but recall what the past year had held for this manager, how desperately she had wanted to be successful from day one, how the past year was an exhausting climb back up from the deepest depths anyone should ever have to go. Halfway through the meeting, my boss walked through the door.

He dropped off his briefcase, said "hello" and made his way to the counter to greet the team. He answered his cell phone and sat at the end of the table. Within a few minutes, he was asking specific questions in the 'drill sergeant' manner for which he was known. I quickly watched my manager crumble. Hands started to shake, she began to ramble while answering basic questions, unable to complete sentences or give specific answers. I coached as much as possible. Beginning the sentence for her: *you know how to figure that, that's when we take the profit*... guiding her through the response by pointing to the specific numbers on the page.

Another phone call and he had to leave. My boss packed up his things, said a few goodbyes, and walked out the front door. How could he be so cruel? He didn't have a clue what he had done. It was just his way of doing business. It was this style of management that got him where he was. His boss was very similar; neither of them ever saw the corpse they left in their wake.

Any person who goes through a life-changing event and makes it to the other side is worth waiting for and working with. I have walked alongside several individuals in my years of management whose lives seemed to be unraveling before them. There exists no handbook that tells us how to handle these times. These are the times that our humanity is put to the test. Business has to be business and decisions need to be made slowly and with great thought. Success in management is based on the relationships we build. Wise managers find ways to balance business with personal tragedy and make choices that best support the business while tending to the needs of the individual.

It was a year into this adventure before life had almost returned to normal. There were a few times of forgetfulness, we called them "blonde-moments". At times, there were questions that caused me to bite my tongue to keep from laughing; questions so simple and obvious that it was difficult to answer intelligently. In those times, it only took a few short seconds for the past adventure to flash in front of me and I would find a way to answer gently and patiently.

There will be times that no one will notice or truly understand the load you are carrying. The reward comes from within; when you truly grasp the difference you have made in a fellow human.

*A side note on HIPA – I've learned a lot about HIPA. I greatly appreciate the concept of "on a need to know basis" and feel it not only relates to illness but so many other areas. I use HIPA in many situations. Most situations fall under HIPA; it is a need to know basis and I do not need to know!*

# When To Say When

So how does one decide it is time to cut the ties, pull the plug, give up or just say this is not working? Undeniably one of the toughest questions any manager has to face.

I recall a co-worker who had let things slide for a very long time. After a manager's training class on accountability, she went back to her store and within two weeks fired almost the entire team. The next two weeks were filled with her frantically trying to fill shifts. The following week, she gave her notice. Knowing when to say when is not a knee-jerk reaction, it needs to be planned out.

If you are struggling to write your schedule, not because you don't have enough people but rather there are team members who aren't meeting expectations; this is a good indication that there are some performance issues needing to be addressed. If Tom doesn't open because he's always late, or Jack gets too focused on tasks, or Ellen creates more work for everyone when she is scheduled, you have issues needing attention.

## Here are a few steps to consider

First you need to ask a few questions:

• Is this individual worth the time and energy it will take to develop them?

• Are others suffering because you need to spend so much time to develop this person?

• If you spent the same amount of time with your best people, where would they be in their development?

Take some time and make a list. On the left side of the paper write the word Asset and on the left side write Liability. Under Asset, list all the qualities, talents and gifts this individual brings to your team. Consider special tasks this individual may have taken on. Does he excel in a specific area of business that would be greatly damaged if he was removed?

Under Liability list the issues, bad habits and any negativity this individual brings to your team. How does the rest of your team feel about this person? Is this person just misplaced and/ or needs to be given tasks that will allow him to excel? Once the list is complete, it should be very clear which side of the page is weighted toward what action you need to take. If the individual is still an Asset but the list of Liabilities seems to be growing, put the list away for a week or so and revisit it. You may need to revisit it several times.

Now that you have come to the conclusion that it is time to move on, there are a few personal questions that need answering.

One needs to take responsibility for one's own leadership:

- How long have I worked with this person?

- Have I been very clear with the expectations, issues or shortcomings?

- How have I communicated these to the individual in question?

- Do I have sufficient documentation?

- Do I have an action plan with clear expectations including time frames that has been signed by myself and the person in question?

- Have I been consistent in my reaction to the situation? Are there others in the group that I have not reacted to?

When you can confidently say "yes" to these questions, you can rest easy that you have done your job. If you are unsure of your answer, bring someone else into the situation, your manager, another manager or your best supervisor. Be very honest with yourself, is it possible that you have become too emotionally attached to this individual and are unable to make a wise business decision on your own?

The secret here is that one never is sure when issues will arise. The reason so many managers become stressed by their teams is because they have let situations go too long and when they are finally fed up, there is no documentation and they have to live through several more months until they can confidently answer "yes" to the above question. As a manager, you have to be consistent from day one. Even if it is your favorite, your strongest employee or your newest. The great ones will appreciate your professionalism, your consistency and your integrity.

Can a poor performer become a strong leader? Most certainly, but it won't happen overnight. The Manager must decide what impact a poor performer will have on the team and business while everyone waits for him/her to improve.

I have worked for companies that could be considered the extreme of the next steps. One company had the practice that someone needed to be terminated, it was as simple as opening the Employee Handbook and randomly pointing to one of those "may be terminated for a first time offense" and wa-la, the termination was complete. Another company did a ton of behind-the-scenes discussion (otherwise known as gripping) but the employee that was not hitting the mark had no clue that they needed improvement. It's difficult to terminate someone who has recently won an undeserving award for excellence.

Terminating is not a fun or easy job and should never be taken lightly. However, not terminating someone who should be terminated sends the wrong message to the team. It shows lack of respect for those who are doing the job well.

Once you believe it is the right decision, and I say believe instead of know – cause rarely will a manager know it's right until it's over – don't look back. Follow your company's procedure for termination and move forward. Be mindful the time between deciding and terminating, this should not be a long drawn out process.

# The Two Minute Termination

The same guy who said, "This job would be easy if it weren't for (those) people," also believed in the two minute termination. He was right. Once the decision to terminate has been made and the paperwork prepared, it's important to move quickly.

Most companies have guidelines on how the actual termination should happen. Some will require a witness. Some may require a district or regional manager to be present. Do what is required but do it quickly. When it comes to the moment of the actual termination, it should go something like this:

Invite the employee to sit down, preferably in the backroom.

Hand him a copy of the termination and read it. Everything you need to say should be on that page. Once you've finished, inform him that they have the right to write a response and that you will need him to sign the document. By signing the document he is not agreeing with it, simply saying that he was giving the document. DO NOT open the door for discussion at this time. Emotions are high right now; yours and his, and discussion will be defensive and could allow you to waiver in your decision.

If he has a key you will need it back. You should ask if he has any belongings in the store and allow him to get them. Thank him for the time he spent with you and follow him to the door.

As the door closes, remember the rest of the staff is watching. How you react when you turn around and what you say in the next few minutes will speak louder than any other time. Be respectful. If you need time to calm your nerves or get fresh air, let the staff know you'll be out for a few minutes. This is neither the time to celebrate nor collapse in front of your team. You have just done one of the toughest parts of your job; don't minimize it by your reaction.

Terminating poor performers sends a very strong message to the rest of your team. It says that you are someone who takes your job seriously, that you respect great employees and won't allow an underperformer to affect other's performance. It says that you are the manager and you will make tough decisions.

Two minutes, that is it. It may take two months to get there, but it should only take two minutes to cross the finish line.

# Part 3
# The Lost Art Of
# Customer Service

# Customer Service

Customer Service is exactly what it sounds like – serving the customers. The degree that you serve your customers is the degree that you will succeed in your business. Great managers look at every aspect of their store from the customer's point of view.

- Is it easy to shop?

- Are the signs easy to understand?

- Are the displays shoppable?

- Is the team warm and welcoming?

# Is your store easy to shop?

Well, is it? Are your customers frustrated or relaxed as they search your store for a certain item? Does the product flow?

There are places within your store that you should think of as the high rent district. These are the areas that are shopped the most. It typically is around your cash register, to the right as you enter your store and directly in front of the entrance. The high rent districts is where you put the merchandise that grabs the customer's attention.

If you have an item that needs a salesperson's assistance in order to sell and you don't have enough staff at all times to ensure someone is present, then this item should be close to the registers. This allows your salesperson to keep a close eye on it and offer assistance even if they are ringing someone else up.

I worked with a company that struggled with product placement within the store. When I asked what made them decide to place their signature item on the left side of the store, opposite the cash register, the visual person basically said, "Cause it's pretty over there." Pretty does not make sales. Pretty doesn't make items easy to shop. Pretty is subjective.

Keep your aisles clean and wide enough for easy shopping. A cluttered sales floor is difficult to shop and maneuver through.

# Are the signs easy to understand?

If you have customers bringing product to the counter to ask, "How much is this?", your promotional signage is failing. Customers should not have to walk around with a calculator to figure out what things cost. Displays should be concise and well marked. We have an outlet mall close to our home. I've shopped a particular store for about five years. It wasn't until recently that I was informed by a new manager that the product is always reduced. The percentage changes from promotion to promotion, but it is never the retail price. This was news to me. Shortly after this new realization, a neighbor mentioned this store and said she loves the clothes but it's too expensive. I asked if she was aware that they are always reduced at least 40%? She looked at me in surprise. Clearly this is a well kept secret – but it shouldn't be.

Set your displays so they are easy to shop and well signed. Then, make sure your team is communicating promotions and sales to the customer. Once when I was shopping at the store where everything is always on sale but no one knows it, I was approached by a salesperson who asked me, "Did you read our sign?" I hesitated for a minute, wondering what sign I may have missed at the front door. "Yes," I said a bit reluctantly. "OK then," she said as she walked away. This was her way of informing the customer of promotions. Never assume that the customer reads and understands all the signs within your store. Informing the customer about a promotion is servicing him. By doing so, you are helping him shop and making it easy for him to purchase the product that you so desperately need him to buy.

## Are the displays shoppable?

We've all see TV shows or commercials where the shopping cart hits a display and it comes tumbling down. Displays should be eye-catching and most importantly, shoppable. Frequently you'll hear the saying, "Stack it high and watch it fly!" in reference to building large displays of product that have depth. Creativity is essential when creating displays, but creativity can at times not be practical.

Once a display is created, step back and look at it from the customer's viewpoint. If it passes that test, step even further back and watch how your customers interact with the display. Does it draw their attention? Do they reach out and pick up an item or is it too intimidating and they are afraid to pick it up. Some displays become works of art that no one wants to mess up.

## Is the team warm and inviting?

Going back to the three Ps, People, Placement, and Product; People are the most important element to the success of your store. Does your team welcome guests? Are they focused on serving rather than selling? One would think that if you changed the focus from sales goals to service goals, that you would not be able to measure the success of the team. The opposite is actually true. Stores that are focused on the customer experience rather than a salesperson's individual sales goal tend to be more successful.

An individual sale's goal can create division and competition between employees. Competition is good but not when 'winning the customer' is the prize. It's the customer that should win, not the salesperson.

# The New Regular Customer

There are some businesses who due to the product sold, have very regular customers. A coffee shop has hundreds of them. A clothing store has a handful, after all, most people don't buy clothes every week. Regular Customers are fun when they return. There's a lot to talk about, a lot to catch up on. It's the ability to have such conversations that allows them to be called a "regular customer".

It is easy for salespeople to be drawn into conversation with our regulars. They can get totally drawn in and ignore other customers. The challenge is to make sure we are serving our regulars while taking every opportunity to create new ones.

Creating regular customers means we've created the *want to*. We've offered them service that they would like to experience over and over again. We've succeeded at making them feel they are a part of the store. Remembering their name is always a plus. Recalling conversations of trips or upcoming events works wonders. When a customer hears, "The last time you were in you were getting ready for your son's wedding." Or "Didn't you go on a trip since the last time you were here?" Remembering and recalling such memories builds a bond of trust. Trust turns your team from salespeople to friends – and who doesn't want to drop in to see friends?

# Is the Customer Always Right?

You only need to work with the public a few short hours to know the answer to this question. NO, the customer is not always right – no one is. However, the customer should always win.

Your team should understand that the quicker they can get to a 'winning' conclusion the better. There is no need for a customer to demand that they talk to a manager if the team is looking for winning solutions.

I took a call one day from an elderly man who was overcharged. After I said my usual phone etiquette greeting, he began to talk. He was mad, he felt he was cheated and overcharged, he had a list of other people who were ready to come and fight his case, he was pissed.

I let him talk for two reasons, he was determined to and I couldn't get a word in anyway. When there came a slight pause in his rant I simply said, "I am so sorry this has happened to you. This is not how we do business. Let me apologize that you have experienced it and that you have been unable to get a resolution before today. I can't change what's happened but I will do my best to fix what I can so that you can move forward."

There was a long silence. When he began to speak, it was as if I were talking to a different individual. Basically he had no more to say, his prepared speech and battle cry were no longer needed. Interestingly, he was no longer concerned about what had happened, he was willing to take the loss as long as it was resolved. He needed to know someone heard him.

Watch customers who are making returns. They are very interesting. Some approach as if they are entering a battle and they are ready to fight. Others bring up the two sisters and their mother who purchased the same item and had the same trouble. They become a bit discombobulated when the person behind the counter smiles and says, "Not a problem. It will take me just a minute to get you your credit." Most start twitching as if they don't know what to do.

Why do we make customer issues difficult? Someone screwed

up and we need to fix it. The longer we draw it out or the more information we give them, the longer the discussion keeps the focus on the screw up. Take care of it quickly and send them on their way. They will remember your great customer service in dealing with a problem, not the problem.

# The Not-So-Bright Customer

You know them. It's the woman who has been waiting in line for 20 minutes at the grocery store and when the person checking her out gives her the total, it dawns on her that she needs to get her checkbook out. Or the man who is number 15 in line at the corner café but it's not until he is asked, "What are you having today?" that he looks at the menu board.

I've dealt with my share of these customers but in all my years of experience, this one still holds the title.

The DO NOT ENTER sign hung on the door and yellow warning tape outlined the frame. I was working in a small café where the women's restroom had experienced a small electrical fire. The old ceiling fan motor had overheated and fell down, landing on the toilet seat which did it's best to ignite, filling the room with smoke and fumes of melting plastic. The restroom was a mess! No lights, the walls were black from the smoke, the toilet seat and floor had huge burn marks. Clearly it was unusable to anyone who saw the mess.

There are three responses to signs that say DO NOT ENTER. The first response is to trust the warning without a doubt and turn and walk away. The second response is to read the sign and trust the warning. However, feeling the need to understand why, these people must open the door in search of the answer. And then there are those who seemingly enter blindly. I've yet to determine if this response is driven by simple distrust or perhaps a feeling of superiority to such warnings. I suppose some simply are unaware that warnings have consequences.

On this particular day, I had been discussing with my co-workers these three responses as it pertained to our "out of order" restroom. During a rather busy time of the day, a customer pulled me aside to inform me that the restroom was a little dirty.

"I'm so sorry," I replied. "I'll get someone in there right away. It is the men's restroom that you are talking about, isn't it?"

"No." was her reply, "The Women's."

With all my might, I kept my composure. "Oh, I am so sorry. We had a fire in the women's restroom and it is not to be used." What was coming out my mouth was so very different than what was going through my mind.

"Oh," was her simple response as she turned and walked away.

I turned around and looked blankly at my co-worker, "You'll never believe what just happened…"

# The Cinnamon Roll

When we weren't setting off the fire alarm in that first café I managed, we were filling the air with aromas that drew our customers in. It was the Cinnamon Roll. It was awesome. The smell of freshly baked cinnamon rolls coming out of the oven is an aroma that forces you to put your head back, close your eyes and walk toward the scent.

We baked cinnamon rolls throughout the day, even if we didn't need them. We needed their aroma. Customers couldn't say no. At 3:00p.m. in the afternoon, at 7:00p.m. just after a movie got out, and most certainly, at 8:30a.m. as people were making their way through the building to get to their office, Cinnamon Rolls – they were our number one marketing tool.

Every store has a cinnamon roll. It is that one thing that gets customers attention and makes them want to buy. It's the cashmere sweater that is 75% off. The blue jeans that are $29.99. It's the newest title release. Sometimes we are lucky enough to have our corporate office provide us with them and sometimes we have to find them. But they are there, you just have to look for them.

When you do find them, it's is the responsibility of you and your team to communicate them to the customer. After all, not everything has a beautiful aroma that draws you in. Cinnamon rolls change, sometimes they are a one day sale and sometimes they are a limited offer. Your team needs to know what the current cinnamon roll is!

These cinnamon rolls need to be easy to find and easy to shop. Placement is as important as their aroma. While managing a children's toy and book store, I stumbled upon a small wooden stringed instrument that I fell in love with. It was easy to learn, easy to play and the sound was amazing. It was like having a small tabletop harp that anyone could learn. Its list price was $59.99. I set one on the front counter so customers could play with it while they were checking out. We instantly had a $59.99 impulse item. Once played, it was sold. It quickly became one of our number one selling items. It was a Cinnamon Roll!

# Creating Energy

Energy, there is no way to measure it but it exists. Walk into any store and you will immediately feel it. Sometimes it's a positive force and sometimes it's a negative force. When it's negative, it repels customers. When it's positive, it will draw them in and make them want to stay awhile. Even better, it will make them want to return.

In the café world, creating positive energy is easy. Since the entire team is high on caffeine, energy should be oozing out of every pour. A café with no or negative energy is a disgrace to the product they are serving. Very little compares to working with a team of highly caffeinated co-workers on the morning shift when everyone is in rhythm. It's a dance. A crazy, wild dance. The rhythm is syncopated, the words are ad libbed, and the audience changes every three minutes.

I recall one morning while working at my store in Naperville, IL. where I caught a glimpse of a businessman pretending to be reading the paper but who was really watching the show behind the counter. We apparently were his morning entertainment. The banter with customers was always amusing but the banter between the team could not be scripted. We laughed, joked, teased, and wished our customers a great day at a neck breaking speed. We believed in the three minute experience. Enter, order, and be served in three minutes. It was a rush and it created an energy that sucked customers in the door.

Creating such a level of energy in a retail environment takes a little more effort. After all, your customer is not coming in for a "pick me up" beverage. None the less, they should feel a positive energy that will inevitably make their day better.

How do we create this positive energy? First, you have to have a team that understands that once they walk out of the Backroom and onto the selling floor, they are on stage. They are to be focused on the customer. Chit-chat can and should happen between co-workers but it must remain positive, professional and appropriate. Discussing a tragic accident that was observed with blood everywhere is not appropriate. Bitching about other employees is not professional. Expressing what a back-assed company they work for is not positive.

There is no room for attitude on the selling floor. When you see it, address it – and not on the floor. A quick trip to the Backroom with a minute conversation: "You look like there's something wrong. Is there?" Wait for an answer. If it is legit, be sympathetic and ask if they need time to pull it together. If it's really serious, offer to send them home; being shorthanded is better than spreading the attitude. If they are going to stay, simply ask, "Are you able to put this aside and be positive on the floor?" Give them a moment and return to the floor.

We've all been in those stores where you are asked 10 times if you need help. I understand when this happens in a very large store such as Home Depot. But when there are three people on the sales floor in a 3,000 square foot store, there is no reason for it. What it tells me is that they are not working as a team. They are not paying attention to who is entering the store and who has been greeted or offered assistance.

A successful store is a welcoming store. The first interaction should be a welcome followed by a generic comment: great day out there isn't it, I love your jacket, how are you this afternoon. That's all. No sales pitch and never ask if they need help when they have just entered the store, they don't know they need help yet, that takes a few moments.

It helps to think of it as if your store is an event, the best event going. You're there because you are the host. You've hired a few people to help you with the event – because it's going to be awesome. You are having a great time, your team is glad they are there and somehow you feel lucky to be there. When the guests arrive (your customers) you want to welcome them. You don't need to sell them on the event – they are already there. Give them time to look around. Give them a chance to feel the positive energy. After they have been there for a few minutes, invite them to the smorgasbord (your product and/or promotion).

Customers expect that most salespeople are there to sell. There is a difference between the way a sales person approaches a customer and how a service person does. The salesperson sees the customer as their sales goal. A service oriented person offers genuine concern and assistance.

When your first approach to the customer is a sincere greeting followed by a generic comment, you remove their defenses. You will see them relax and the wall of protection against pushy salespeople crumbles. Some don't know what to do. They had their "NO" speech all prepared, you've just changed the game. On the second interaction you are explaining the promotion or the newest product or the buy of the day or what we could call that day's Cinnamon Roll without expecting anything from them. You again have for a second time made them feel welcome and comfortable. By the third interaction, you are best friends and they are so glad you invited them to this fantastic event. They trust you and want your expert opinion. They will spend money, they will be back, and they will certainly tell their friends.

Positive energy is contagious. Positive energy draws in positive energy and repels negative. One of the highest compliments an employee can give a manger is the one that says, "I love coming to work. It's the place where all the yuckiness of the day stays outside and we get to escape in here." Does your team feel that way? Do you feel that way? Do your customers feel as if they have been part of an awesome event?

There is no room for negativity on the selling floor. Personal dilemmas should not be shared with the customer. A customer does not need to hear that the person ringing up their items was just evicted and their ex-husband is a jerk. Those are discussions for the backroom not for the selling floor. They may have just been evicted and their ex-husband is a jerk, but sharing such personal information is inappropriate. It turns the focus on the salesperson and not on the customer, which is where it belongs.

It's all about the customer. From the minute they walk in the door to the second they leave. It's an event that they have had the privilege to attend and while they were there, they had the honor of meeting a great group of people who they now consider their friends – your team.

After all, selling a customer what they really want is servicing them.

# Merchandising Speaks Volumes

Do we merchandise our stores to make them look beautiful or to make it inviting for our guests? Both should be happening but *inviting to our guests* is primary. It should be effortless to shop at your store. Don't ask them to work to get an item off the top shelf or read the sign or not know where the line starts. You do not pay them to work at your store, they are paying you.

Checkout lines should be clearly marked. Promotions should be well written and easy to understand. Product should be well displayed for easy access. A pyramid of boxes may look appealing, but how does anyone buy one without the pyramid collapsing? Clothes hung at the top of the wall should be there for presentation, but a customer should not need a ladder to select a sweater they want to buy. When I am the customer, I refuse to shop places that make it difficult to shop. I don't care how cute the blouse is hanging 10 feet in the air, if you are asking me to work to get that blouse, I quit. I'll go somewhere else.

There is an art to merchandising. Not everyone can make displays look great. If you can find someone on your team with such a gift, use them. Have them share their knowledge with the rest of the team.

# A Customer Service Story

A few years ago, I found myself in a dressing room at GAP just outside Denver CO. I had a 50% off coupon and was in need of a few things. My daughter joined me for the first hour or so, filling my room with all sorts of finds. Shortly after she left, there was a knock on the dressing room door. I opened it to find a young saleswoman, arms overflowing with denim, "I brought you every style and in a couple sizes – thought you would like to try them on." I thanked her, she left, I closed the door, sat down and began to sob.

You see, seven weeks earlier we had received a call that our daughter was being airlifted to a Denver hospital because her water broke 26 weeks into the pregnancy. Within hours, my husband and I were on a plane to Denver, where I remained for the next seven weeks to be with her and care for my 18 month old grandson. I had been mom, grandma, advisor, cook, housekeeper, diaper changer. I had sat through heart surgery, brain scans, brain surgery, blood transfusions, hospital visits, the list is endless. I had missed Thanksgiving at home and all the holiday preparations for Christmas. I spent every hour of every day serving others – AND for what felt was the first time in seven weeks – someone was SERVING me. Yes, it was denim, but it was so much more. It took a good 30 minutes for me to gain my composure and make my way to the checkout. That 20-something salesclerk with an arm full of blue jeans will never know what she meant to me.

Customer service is about service, the result is the sale. If we focus on the service, it will never grow old; we'll never tire of it. If we focus on service, we will keep every customer and the rewards will be great.

# Part 4
# Personal Development

# Personal Development

We now begin to focus on the most important part of being a manager, YOUR personal development. It isn't likely you will find this listed on your company's Top Ten list of priorities – Sam's Personal Development Plan. Companies like to train, but rarely do they spend the time and energy to develop. For most managers, personal development has to be sought after. This means it's your responsibility. It's obvious that you take this seriously since you have picked up this book. I congratulate you on taking steps to improve your style and your skills.

In this section we are going to look at your style of management and what has and will influence your style.

# The Multidimensional Manager

Your style of management has undoubtedly had a variety of influences. Your boss, the culture of the companies that you've worked, your successes and failures along the way have all contributed to who you have become as a manager.

Who you are as an individual also plays an important part in your style. Someone who is naturally honest and strives for a high level of integrity in their personal life will bring those attributes to their position. Just as someone who manipulates or finds the need to control everything in their personal life will most likely do the same to their team and superiors.

People come in various degrees of dimensions. Those that

are self-absorbed are one-dimensional, while those who are continually aware of themselves and the world around them are multidimensional. A one-dimensional manager is one who is continually aware of how he is treated or mistreated, but is unable to look at the effect he has on others. These individuals will attend training classes and management development seminars, inevitably relating what they have heard to how their peers or boss manages, but rarely will be able to identify their own areas of opportunity.

The managers that I enjoy working with the most, and believe are the most successful, are the multidimensional managers. They continually look for ways to understand their boss, themselves and the way they affect those who report to them. At times, it would be much easier not to care what the effect of our actions has on others, but that a good manager does not make.

It takes effort to step back and look honestly at the effect you have on your team and your business. A multidimensional manager will do just that on a regular basis. Decisions are thought through; this manager does not make or respond to knee jerk reactions. It is difficult for a multidimensional manager to be part of a team made up of one-dimensional peers; it quickly becomes emotionally draining. It is extremely difficult for a multidimensional manager to work for a one-dimensional boss.

I am reminded of an old proverb that says, *"A pupil is not above his teacher; but everyone, after he has been fully trained, will be like his teacher."* As a teacher, it is empowering to think that one has the ability to reproduce strong skills, great knowledge, and positive character traits. This proverb promises that a student who is trained correctly will become like the teacher.

There is a side to this old proverb that has also concerned me over the years. If a student will become like their teacher, what happens if the teacher isn't someone one should desire to be like? I have had the opportunity to work for a few individuals that I had no desire to emulate. I pondered this proverb; fearful that I would become like them and wondering how I could ever rise above the management style in which I found myself being managed. If, in fact, I was destined to become like my teacher - this proverb became more of a curse than a promise. Is it ever possible to break the chain? Is it possible to actually become better than the teacher or in other words to rise above?

Rising above takes determination not to settle. Rising above requires patience, wisdom and integrity to see beyond the obvious and a willingness to walk into the unknown. It also requires the understanding that if the proverb is true, you as the student will become like your teacher. It is also true and even more importantly, your students will become like you.

To fully grasp this concept is to fully understand the importance a manager plays in the life of their employees. In doing so, we realize that management suddenly moves from *an easy job I can do until I find what I am really looking for* to understanding that I have the power to effect another human being.

There are very few positions in this world that allow us to have such an effect on others. A schoolteacher can mold, teach and impart knowledge; a manager has the opportunity to model and teach skills that can be used in every aspect of life. Great management skills are transferable not only in business but also in real life. Self-discipline, integrity and great conversational skills are essential elements in our day to day lives.

On the flip side, a bad manager can be almost as detrimental as a bad parent. Most individuals that walk into a job with attitude do so because of the baggage that was created by a past manager. The walls of defense are already up and they are anticipating that they will not be respected as an individual. If you listen to the conversation of a group of people who are being poorly managed, you will quickly see that work invades their entire life. When they go out as a group, all they can discuss is work and these conversations tend not to be positive. When they are in a non-work environment, work seems to be the topic of conversation.

Listen to a group of people who are being well managed and work stories are about funny, crazy customers or situations. They have the ability to laugh at themselves and the silly mistakes that were made. Most importantly, they have a lot to talk about that is not work related.

This position called manager is powerful. In the hands of someone who respects that power – amazing results will occur. In the hands of someone who is not ready or incapable of handling that level of responsibility, it becomes explosive with sometimes damaging results.

Rising above creates dimension. Those who grasp the idea of rising above are able to survive in any work environment. They remain calm under pressure and are able to handle almost any situation. The ability to rise above comes with knowledge of what 'above' looks like and how far 'above it is'.

Rising above does not mean you are an elitist, feeling some sense of superiority. Rising above is a sign of emotional maturity. It's living your life with high standards for yourself that allows you to not get trapped in the muck.

*"A pupil is not above his teacher; but everyone, after he has been fully trained will be like his teacher."* As a manager you find yourself at both ends of this proverb. You are being taught and you are also teaching. If you find yourself not wanting to become like your teacher, you will need to learn to rise above. But more importantly, you have students and you have the power to develop work habits, disciplines and ethics that will last them a lifetime.

171

# Personal Development
# Personal Style

There is a huge difference between training a manager and developing a manager. Training a manager simply provides information about the job that is to be performed. Developing a manager focuses on the skills needed to perform the tasks required. This includes skills such as financial competence, people skills, operational integrity and personal development. Most companies pride themselves on training their managers; few spend the time and energy to develop them.

Our first look at developing management skills is to define what type of manager you are. I hate being pigeonholed as much as the next person, but I do realize that there are similarities in the way we approach our jobs. I worked for a company who prided itself in the fact that every year they put their management team through the newest personality evaluation testing. After the tests were scheduled, administered and completed, we waited for the results which were usually delivered at a group gathering such as a conference or seminar. We would eagerly read through the results making comments of agreement, dislike and sarcasm. After the initial shock of seeing oneself in an outline, or in some cases an actual book, we waited eagerly for the development to begin. It never did. By the time the results had been delivered, someone in HR had attended a different seminar introducing that year's *hottest test* and preparations were already being made for us to be re-evaluated. There sits in the back corner of my closet a box of test results that categorize me in a multitude of ways.

Learning about ourselves only helps if we actually *learn* about ourselves. With that knowledge, we are able to better ourselves. Knowledge unused is worthless. Being evaluated and categorized can better us, but it can also stunt us. Every character trait and every skill can evolve; they can become stronger and more defined and in some cases, if these skills are not used properly, can deteriorate. We are in control of who we are and who we become. Understanding who we are and why we respond in a certain way allows us to sift through the junk to find the gold.

The key element to evaluating ones skills is what we do with the results of the evaluation. There is nothing more frustrating than speaking with someone who can list off all their limitations or disabilities, such as ADD, poor time management, or shyness but never go to the next phase of learning how to use these limitations or change them. Knowing truly is half the battle, what you do with that knowledge will determine if you are going to win or lose the battle.

There is something very impressive when a manager can say, "I really struggle with time management – so I've created a great schedule that keeps me on task." Or "I have ADD so I know I'm all over the place, but I've surrounded myself with very organized people who help me stay focused." Personally, I have difficulty remembering numbers such as percentages, comps and actual sales. I had the privilege to work with a guy that could not only recall all of his financial numbers but everyone else's as well. If we were ever in a meeting together and I was unable to recall my percentages, I simply glanced over to him and he would fill in the blank. Since it seemed unrealistic to think he would be at my beckoning call, I decided I needed to create an aid for myself. I now have a binder that contains all the essential figures I need, it's well organized for easy reference. This binder accompanies me to every meeting and lays open in front of me during every conference call. I know my limitation and I've come up with a solution. There has never been a situation when asked about numbers and I've pulled out my binder that someone said, "That's unacceptable!" Actually it's just the opposite. Typically I get asked, "Do you have my numbers?"

It is essential to know and understand your strengths and

weaknesses, but it is more important to know how to use them and how to compensate for them. Remember, knowing is only half the battle. We are going to begin by looking at four basic management styles. You will find that these are very general in their descriptions. They are intended to be so. They were developed to be a guide – not a label. Styles change. Our personal style is influenced by our experiences, our past and our goals. Managers find themselves moving from one style to another and perhaps even back again. What is important is to understand what effects these four styles have on your business, your team, your career and your position.

# Management Styles

After years of training managers and managing multi-units, I began to see similarities in management styles which ultimately translated into similarities in results. As much as we would like to think we are all unique and approach our positions with a new point of view, there are great similarities. In many cases, the results became predictable based on the style of manager. In a world where variables outweigh the constant, any level of predictability is welcomed.

As I began to list general character traits, I also began to make lists of typical results. I then tested this theory and to my amazement found it to be accurate. They have been used to assist a struggling manager to improve and a burned out manager to face facts. When faced with the task of assembling a team, these profiles assist in establishing a diverse group that work well together.

# These are the A B C & Ds of Managers
## The "A" Manager

The A Manager is one who comes to the table with a wealth of experience. New managers rarely fall into this category since it takes a great deal of time to develop strong management skills. This is the visionary and planner. She is always looking ahead. She knows the details of the next promotion and understands what it will take to execute it. This manager fills empty wall space with lists, calendars and training tools. Every act has a purpose and nothing falls through the cracks. In fact, she will put in place several layers of safety nets to avoid any disaster.

People Skills are very strong and well developed. This individual has learned to be very discerning when it comes to building a team. She can read employees quickly and with accuracy. She is not afraid to hire raw talent because she knows the new employee can develop it. She is respected by the team she manages. There is a great difference between being liked and being respected. Some managers can be very well liked but not at all respected. Likewise an individual can be respected but not well liked. There is danger in both. At first, respect comes because a person holds the title of manager. This type of entitled respect needs to become earned respect. Our A's know how to quickly gain respect because of their title and have the ability to turn this into earned respect due to their personal performance in a very short period of time.

This manager is rarely without a strong team. Great people attract great people. When all other managers are out recruiting staff, this individual has more applications than she can possibly ever need. Usually, the only time employees leave is due to internal promotions; this can occur frequently due to the strong ability to develop skills. When it comes to the team that she manages, it is very clear that individual growth and development is first priority. The standard is high and this manager is willing and able to provide the team with the tools needed to achieve the goal. The team understands that they will be held accountable and treated fairly.

The operations of the business are examples to all. Standards, promotions and introduction of new product are executed flawlessly. The team understands the expectations and takes ownership in the outcome. When others are complaining that they do not have enough time to accomplish workloads, the A Manager is asking for more responsibilities.

Training is typically a strong suit for this individual and their team. However, not all A's are great trainers. Generalizations are commonly made that because someone excels in a position, they should inevitably be able to train others. Training is a skill set unto its own. Another common mistake for these A Managers is to assume that they are promotable. A great teacher doesn't always make a great principal. A great manager doesn't always make a great District Manager.

Financially this individual runs a very tight ship. Profitability, year on year increases exceed company averages. Financial planning is part of their everyday life. When goals are missed, they are not looking back to find excuses for not hitting the goal, instead they are looking months ahead to make sure it won't happen again.

## Managing the A Manager

A Managers can be long-term managers and are usually promotable. They are also very challenging. This group needs to be stimulated - status quo does not cut is. The carrot on the stick does not work either. They are too intelligent to be sucked into false promises and unrealistic goals. They require respect from those they manage, their peers and superiors. They have integrity and demand it from their company.

The A's are the ones who are in control. Work seems effortless. They are driven by success and love to be the winner. Juggling 20 balls is more fun than juggling 10. It's not the juggling that is rewarding; it is the amount being juggled. Boredom comes quickly and with boredom comes lack of focus. When there is lack of focus, personal creativity is engaged to fill in the gap and this can lead to some moments of brilliancy or catastrophe. Stress levels vary and most of the stress is self-imposed due to their great personal drive.

The A Manager requires very little hands-on managing. Picture the bumpers used when children are bowling; the A

Manager simply needs someone to place bumpers along the way to keep her focused. She provides the energy, knowledge and motivation to succeed.

## The "B" Manager

The B Manager is the perfectly balanced manager: Responsible, respected and centered.

People skills are strong and always developing. The B Manager builds fun teams. The team respects this manager from the beginning because he is transparent, engaging and likable. He understands the balance between developing a team and developing individuals. He also knows that development and accountability go hand in hand.

These managers are strong trainers. They are motivated by the challenge of training others. Finding the right learning and teaching styles needed to develop an individual is as much fun for this group as the actual training process. These managers are endlessly creating new ways to present material. Because of their strong ability to train and the success they have in training, they have a tendency to hire individuals that may not be a solid fit because they are confident that they are able to train. "I can teach them to do this job" is their hiring motto.

Operations of the business are strong; meeting and usually exceeding expectations is the norm. No one is overstressed or overworked. When taking on additional responsibilities, this manager is never without volunteers because he have gained the trust and respect of his team.

The business financials are solid in a B Manager's business. Goals are carefully set. This manager knows when to use a goal for the purpose of development, to motivate, or strictly for financial results. If given a choice, this manager will choose developing his team over achieving a financial goal. This can come across as being not engaged or uninterested, when actually it is simply putting people ahead of business results.

The B Manager has achieved balance between life and work. Because of this balance he is able to build fun, strong teams who also understand the importance of balancing work and personal life. Stress is created when the balance between work and personal life is interrupted.

## Managing the B Manager

B Managers keep a company strong. It is where all the time and energy should be placed in order to keep and further develop these individuals. This group is made up of smart, solid players. Their input is invaluable. They are not easily pulled in one direction or another due to their deep understanding and respect for balance in all areas. These managers will also be the first to see the flaws or potential roadblock occur in company promotions, restructuring or other company driven changes. Because of this, it is important that this group is given an avenue to communicate these foreseen obstacles.

# The "C" Manager

The C Manager is typically the new manager who is lacking in experience. However, it can also be the manager who has been in position too long and is simply going through the motions. In this case, these managers typically have built-up bitterness or frustration toward the company and a lack of respect for how things are done. This can also be an individual that has never had anyone take the time to develop their management skills or have not taken the initiative to seek personal development on their own.

People Skills are lacking mostly due to lack of experience but can also be lack of desire. There is very little accountability of their teams because there are very few expectations communicated. Ironically, these managers do have expectations but are either afraid or ineffective in communicating them.

The C Manager hires individuals based on need or the applicant's availability. These managers are typically understaffed and fill positions with warm bodies rather than seeking out strong applicants that will better the team. It is their own insecurities that force them to avoid hiring individuals with strong personalities for fear of actually having to be a leader. Training is very inconsistent primarily due to lack of time, especially for new employees. Lack of time forces these managers to throw new employees into positions expecting them to learn as they go.

Operationally the C Manager's business lacks standards, the

ability to meet deadlines and executes promotions. This, in addition to the poorly trained team, will greatly affect financial results. There is undoubtedly low or negative energy within themselves and their team.

The C Managers live in a world of stress; rarely feeling in control of their business or their personal life and can quickly fall into the abyss of "reasons and excuses" why they are unable to reach a goal.

# Managing the C Manager

C Managers are in desperate need of a strong mentor for several reasons. If this is a new manager who lacks experience, he needs someone to walk alongside to assure that those new experiences are drawn upon to learn new lessons. A strong mentor will also be able to share his own personal experiences for additional learning.

If this is a manager who has never been developed or has never taken the initiative to seek out personal development on her own, she will require retraining in most of her management skills. Wiping the slate clean and starting over is very challenging and if not handled properly can cause conflict.

Lastly, if this is a manager who is reaching burnout, it takes a strong mentor to help her become re-energized or bring her to the point of acknowledging the burnout and make necessary changes before she is forced to leave. A strong mentor will also be able to assist in managing the individuals on the C Manager's team. The manager who is reaching or has reached burnout will have a great effect on her team, it is the responsibility of the mentor to step in when needed to protect the team. The goal is to move these managers into the B group rather than watch them fall into the D group. The C Manager will only last a year as a C and in most cases this is too long of time. Ultimately, there is one of two conclusions to their career; they will either quit or be terminated.

## The "D" Manager

Caution lights, red flags and sirens should instantaneously go off when coming in contact with the D Manager. This manager is clearly in the wrong position. He may be very new and green in his management skills, obviously promoted too quickly. He may have been a C Manager who has fallen into complete burnout. Or, perhaps he is the individual who thinks that management is a mindless job that a monkey could do. The D Managers need to be dealt with quickly with clear expectations and deadlines. These managers will have a huge negative effect on their teams and in some situations, scar them for life.

Understaffed; zero application flow; people walking off the job with no notice; working extra long hours are all the theme of the day. It is a continual cycle with no end in sight. Great employees can spot a D Manager a mile away and will never agree to work under such a person. As a result, these already burned out or overwhelmed managers will hire whatever they can find, which keeps them in the cycle of always hiring. Training will happen once there are finally enough people to write a schedule, it's sink or swim - baptism by fire. This manager is out of control and is unable to repair the damage.

Operationally and financially . . . there are no systems in place, operations do not exist and financials are hemorrhaging. Every aspect of the business is in utter chaos.

Stress and tension is measurable. These managers require much more than a strong mentor; they require a strong, authoritative boss. Someone who can balance the stern, direct disciplinary actions required to deal with this manager and protect the team for which they are responsible. A manager who has fallen so far down can do great damage to their team. Sadly these managers build teams consisting of teenagers who are in their first jobs or dysfunctional employees who have issues with authority. It is not uncommon to find a group of friends all working together for a D Manager. Since no responsible, balanced employee will work under this level of manager, a team is built by employee referrals. Bad employees will always refer bad employees. The poor work conditions created by a D Manager will taint a young employee's view of the work place for the rest of his/her working life.

# Who Are You?

As you read through these styles, where do you find yourself?

- If you found yourself falling between two styles, which one would you like to be?

- What style would your boss say you are? What style is he – after all he, too, is a manager?

- What style would your peers say you are?

- What style would your team say you are?

- Do you see yourself currently moving up to the next category or sliding back one?

- Where do you want to be?

Now it's time for a little free advice. Figuring out which management style best fits you is the first step. The second is understanding how you fit into a company. After all, you are not an island. You have people to manage and have to report to others. Understanding how others perceive you allows you to become dimensional.

## Tough talk to the D Manager

Let's be honest...What the hell are you doing? Quit it and get on with life. Either you are committed or you are not. You are a liability to your company, your peers and your team. If someone is not riding your ass, shame on them.

Can you turn this around? Of course you can, but it will take much more effort than you have been willing to give. How do I know this? Because you have allowed yourself to be at the bottom. You have given up. You have not used the tools provided. You have become complacent and are numb to the fact that you are hurting the people around you.

Stop taking advantage of your company. Stop playing games. Stop manipulating the situation. Either start to do the job you have been hired to do or go find another job.

If you decide to turn it around, you are heading towards an uphill battle. Most likely you have lost the respect of your peers, your team and your supervisor. Your first step is to regain their trust which will take a very long time. Don't fool yourself, your current performance is going to follow you for some time, you won't wake up with a clean slate.

The greater concern is your team. If they have stayed under your management, they most likely need to be terminated. They have learned too many bad habits and will most likely not be able or willing to get back to standards. It is highly unlikely that you have great employees working for you. My guess is that you have lost anyone with high standards and the ability to help you build a new team.

I am being as direct as I can possibly be. I assume that no one has had any straightforward discussions with you at this point of your career. Bosses who have honest conversations with their employees prevent individuals from falling this far down. If you are the manager who thinks management is an easy job and you'll do it until your real job comes along, there is no doubt that you are in the wrong position...move out. Go find the job that suits you. Finally, stop blaming the company, your boss or your customers for your current state. They may have added to the situation, but when it comes to the type of manager you are, you must take responsibility for it. There are great managers in bad companies just as there are bad managers in great companies. Take an honest look at yourself and your performance and decide if it's time to move out or get back in the game.

## Do you find yourself a C Manager?

If you are a C Manager, you need to understand why. Were you a B Manager at some point? If so, how long ago? Looking back, is there a point where you can see you changed? What happened that caused such a change in your performance? Has the job become too routine for you? Are you simply bored with your current position? Do you want to improve or are you done? Be honest.

Were you a D Manager and have improved your performance? If so, you deserve a huge pat on the back. Your work is not done, however. You have a long way to go to become a B Manager. It is possible, but it will take much effort on your behalf. Set your goals and make them measurable. Surround yourself with people who will keep you on track. You need people who will encourage, keep you accountable and support you in the right ways. This is NOT your team. Your team is there to be managed by you, not teach you to do your job. Put some separation between you and those who like to complain, you can't afford their negativity. Most of all, build your team with the best individuals you can find. You don't need anyone who requires a lot of your time or energy right now; YOU are the only project on the list. You have to fix you before you can fix someone on your team.

Are you a new manager and struggling through your first year? For most new managers, you are where you should be; You also have a lot of work to do. The first year is the most important. I have often told new managers that Experience is all they lack. If I could bottle Experience and give it to you, I would. Unfortunately, Experience must be obtained with time. Focus on improving your management skills, remove all other distractions. This is the time for you to put your personal stamp on your business, your team and your results. Do not allow yourself to be pulled in more directions than what is expected in your current position. Once your team is in place, your results are something to be proud of, and you are established as a solid manager, there will be plenty of time to move beyond your four walls.

If you were a B Manager and have found yourself falling backwards, you need to take an honest look at your performance. Are you bored with your current position? If so, why? Are you able to pull yourself out and become the B Manager again? Are you close to burn out? Is it time for a job change? Take time to do some soul searching. Ask a trusted peer for input. Have a very honest conversation with your boss. Ask the tough questions and be open to their feedback.

If you find yourself stuck in a downward spiral, you have a choice to make; either it's over or you are ready to move forward. My challenge to you is to make your decision quickly. Don't let it get drawn out...it could get messy. At some point, you will need to be held accountable for your performance. Also, take into consideration the team of people who report to you. Are you being the best boss they have ever had? Are you an example of a great manager? That is what they deserve. That is what they signed up for. Either you will be that manager or you won't. If you decide not to be...move on...it's time to go.

But, if you feel ready to move forward, stay focused, you can turn it around. You have experience on your side and you know what it is like to be the B Manager...go for it. Be the best.

## WARNING to the A Manager

First of all, you must realize that you can be very overwhelming to others. Your experience exceeds most of your peers and perhaps your boss. Your delivery can come across as condescending to others, even if you are not trying to do so. This is not to say you should not join in conversation, just be aware of those around you. Rather than having all the right answers - try asking the right questions to allow others to make their own conclusions.

When it comes to your team, you are light years ahead of this group as well. The majority of your team may be there for a paycheck on their way to their real life. Find ways to communicate information that keeps them motivated; too much information may be above their understanding and interest level. Find the handful of employees that want to learn and teach them but don't overwhelm them. Keep it simple and allow them to process at their own speed.

Find ways to keep yourself challenged. Keep your own charts and spreadsheet. Create your own set of goals and file them under personal growth.

When it comes to a career path, you may find yourself feeling as if you are a job hopper. Most likely you are. Because you learn easily and take ownership quickly, you conquer most jobs faster than most. Challenge yourself when making career decisions: Is this really the right place for you or is it just easy?

When A Managers find themselves unchallenged, it is essential for them to have a fulfilling personal life. Allow your creativity and extra energy to be used outside of your job. Most A Managers will never be fulfilled by their current position. Do not expect your position to meet all your needs. Allow it to be the job that gives you the means or time to have a life outside of work. It is a very healthy way to live and will help you learn to enjoy what you are doing and not tire of it quickly. You may actually find that you can just have fun at work while your drive is channeled into your personal life.

Be the best. Strive after excellence. Excellence does not always equal the highest scores or the most sales. Excellence does not mean you were the first to have checked everything off the list. Excellence is a standard that is driven by your character. If you are able to teach your team the importance of striving for excellence, you will be teaching them life lessons. Striving for excellence will help to balance your drive, your expectations and your energy. At the end of each day, striving for excellence allows you to turn off the lights, lock the doors and be motivated to face the next day.

# B Proud

Be proud to be a B Manager. You are most likely in the right position. Stay the course. Do not get distracted by what others are doing or not doing. Your life is usually in balance, keep it that way. When you find yourself becoming stressed, take a step back and figure out what's out of sync. A few quick adjustments and you'll be back on course.

Because you are a natural at this job, it can become routine. Challenge yourself by adding more diversity to your team. Since you find yourself well staffed, take time to interview several individuals even if you don't need them at the moment. What are you looking for? Someone who will push you and your team to a new level.

If you enjoy training, find someone on your team that you can begin to train in other aspects of the business. Most managers only have the desire and time to train on the basics; branch out. Find an area of your business that no one is tapping into. The more information you can give your team, the more knowledgeable they become. That added knowledge puts them on the path to becoming an expert. Experts are less likely to leave. Experts also take great pride in their knowledge and will, in turn, share it with their peers and customers.

Keep focused on the present. Do not fall into the trap of always wondering "what is next?" Your abilities, talent and success speak for themselves. The B Manager is never without cheerleaders. Remember, your team can be your greatest admirers, don't let them down. Most likely, you have earned the respect of your peers and superiors. Leverage that respect. Don't be afraid to speak up. If something is broken, point it out and be part of the solution. Every company has areas that need improvement, find opportunities to be on the 'improvement team'.

As a B Manager, you are the core of the company. You are what makes your company successful. With great pride, you should be able to say, "I am a manager".

# Bringing the Past with Us

Part of understanding our style, and determining what and who we want to be as managers, is to understand the impact previous managers have had on us. I love hiring young people who have never worked before for one reason; I get to be their first manager. I get a clean slate and am able to set the stage for them for the rest of their lives. It is very rare to hire a manager with no previous experience. All managers come with past experiences.

Three men with history …

# TED

Ted was in his late 30's. He had many years of supervisory type positions but never a store manager. He was not the primary income for his family; that position belonged to his wife. When I am interviewing for manager positions, I like involving several other managers as part of the interview process. I feel it is very helpful in deciding who would fit on the team and who connected to different manager types. This is a great help during the training process and also helps the newcomer feel connected before the first day. This particular individual had met with several managers who all raved about his personality, experience and energy. How could I let this one go? I set up the final interview and met Ted late one afternoon.

I have done more interviews than I would like to remember and usually, I can put someone at ease quickly, but not this one. He was nervous. Sixty minutes of nervous. I agreed that he had a ton of experience and on paper was a perfect fit but I could not figure out the nerves. After the interview, I went back to those who had previously spoken with him and again received rave reviews. It took awhile to realize but every manager Ted had an encountered was also a male. My business sense said to bring him onboard and see what he could do. My feminine side said to watch carefully; it was possible that Ted may struggle working for a woman.

I offered Ted the position and he accepted with great

enthusiasm. I planned my first few meetings with Ted carefully. For the first couple meetings, I made sure that there was another manager present. The conversation was very thought out. I chose my words carefully. There was some joking, a lot of discussion and I was sure to ask several times for opinions of both the experienced manager and Ted, always being very careful not to react too dramatically to any response. It took only a few meetings until I could see an obvious change in Ted's comfort level; within a month he was much more at ease interacting with me.

# JOHN

Most managers struggle with holding others accountable. If they don't, they are usually tyrants at work. John was one who didn't like holding anyone but himself accountable.

John was in his mid 40's and he was a pushover. Anything his team asked for, they got; time off, more shifts, short shifts, long shifts, come in late, come in early, does not clean bathrooms or mop floors. You name it and John's team had requested it.

He was working himself to death, picking up shifts, covering for someone who at the last minute bought concert tickets, when they knew they were scheduled to work. When John was working, he was breaking a sweat the entire time, while his team assisted by informing him of all the unfinished tasks they were leaving for him to complete.

John's store was clean, his Backroom was perfectly organized and his financial results had glimpses of perfection. But I knew that this was a one-man show and John needed to stop being the busy bee, begin to delegate and really become the manager of his business.

We had several discussions about this issue. I would ask about someone's performance and he would give me a few excuses and reasons why that particular individual was not able to do the task. We would talk about holding people accountable and he would say he felt more like the parent, it was difficult to hold them accountable but he would try harder. Try harder was not the answer I wanted. John was trying as hard as he possibly could and was working even harder.

# PAUL

Paul was very up front and honest. If he had to change his schedule, he would immediately call me and let me know the details. If there was an error in his paperwork, he would email me with what had happened and how he took care of it. At first, it was somewhat refreshing to have this much detailed information from a new manager. As time went by, I realized that this was not only coming out of his integrity but it was also being driven by past experience.

Paul had worked for a few female managers that were less than exemplary. I am referring to those managers that carry their emotions over their head like a giant helium balloon, and you never know when it may get too close to the ceiling and explode all over you. There are many male managers that fall into the same category but typically they are much more consistent; they are always explosive. Female managers that have not mastered the talent of consistency are much more damaging. What might be seen as acceptable one day, may get you fired the next. It all depends on how close that balloon is to the ceiling. This reactive behavior prevents employees from becoming competent in their decisions. Basically, employees become scared children who want to please mom but are not sure what actions will result in acceptance or punishment.

At first, most of Paul's emails and voice mails began with, "I want to let you know what happened just in case someone complains..." It took me awhile to realize that he really was not concerned if I knew the details or not; he was much more concerned that I may hear about the situation. His concern was that the balloon may be too close to the ceiling and he was wanting to avoid it popping!

Ted, John and Paul's reactions to me were based on what they had each experienced in the past. Ted had been beaten up and humiliated by a female manager, who used her title to gain respect but never earned it on her own. John had worked for someone who was very inconsistent in her own expectations, what was funny one day was a write up the next. Favorites were given privileges but no one knew for sure what the formula was for becoming a favorite. He learned to never ask for help or show any signs that there may be issues. John had learned to be a one man show as a way to ward off his boss's inconsistent behavior. Paul had experienced the 'someone told me so it must be true' manager that left him always on guard and made sure he covered his tracks even before he made them.

It took time and a lot of carefully planned meetings for Ted and I to have a very healthy relationship. We could joke, discuss and even got to the point of disagreeing without making him tremble.

I deflated John's image of being a father figure to staff. I asked him one day, how he would handle his own children, if they never picked up their rooms or finished homework or completed the responsibilities they were given around his home? He immediately had a response, which included a plan followed up with disciplinary actions. It did not take him long to connect that he was not being a father figure by letting things slide. A good father holds his children accountable and teaches them to be responsible. John also came to see that some of his behavior was based not on his ability but his past experiences. John and I worked together for several years and when it was time to part, I remember so clearly our conversations. "I have never worked for a boss like you, thanks…" unable to finish his sentence he turned and walked away.

Paul continued to struggle with the fear of the reaction. Finally, after the coaching and mentoring had not seemed to have made a difference, we had a very honest conversation:

Paul, how long have you worked for me?

A year.

Have you ever seen me blow up?

No.

Paul, have I ever come to you and accused you of something that someone else informed me of, assuming that you are guilty?

No.

Paul, have I ever assumed something had happened without first asking you to give me your side of the story?

No.

Then what makes you so confident that it is going to happen?

No answer.

It did not take Paul long after that conversation to connect that his past experiences were having an effect on our relationship. There were still times that he became very concerned that I might hear something, but a gentle "Paul...have I ever...", brought him back to reality.

In management, we can never forget that every person who reports to us brings with them past experiences of previous bosses; some good, some bad and some that have scared and wounded them deeply. It can be very easy to rise above such past experiences; however, it is not always easy to gain the complete trust of those who have been deeply wounded.

Female managers are confronted with stereotypes that most men don't deal with. Females in management need to rise above experiences of past female bosses, those experiences that have left what was once a confident employee, afraid of the balloon exploding. They may also need to rise above past experiences with over reactive mothers, angry schoolteachers and nasty girls from Jr. High.

There was a time, I thought that anyone could do this job but I have come to realize and admit that this is a tough job. No one comes to you with a clean slate, everyone brings with them past experiences. Frequently, we have to rise above situations we did not even know existed; Consistency, honesty and, most of all, integrity are key in these situations. You may encounter someone that you are unable to help overcome a past experience, but you can give him a new example of a boss that strives to rise above.

# R-E-S-P-E-C-T

It was a week before Christmas. I had been responsible for opening and running two new districts and for the past three years, had been the only manager to whom these two remote districts had reported. The area was not easy to get to, preventing them from being on the list of stores included in corporate visits. Corporate visits are very important when done correctly. They have the potential of allowing store managers to show off. It had been more than three years and I was scheduling the first official cooperate visit to this area.

I knew the day would be tight. Hundreds of miles to make the full circle, but if we stayed on track, we could see everyone I had promised to visit. Each manager was well prepared, they had done their homework. The stores looked great and the excitement was high. It was also my intent to be able to wish each team a happy holiday. As long as we held to the schedule, we would be able to get back to the big city in time for flights back home.

We started out early and to my amazement were on time. In the front seat with myself was my direct report, who was new to the company, and in the back seat was her direct report. I was determined this was going to be an enjoyable 12 hours together, and I knew my team of managers was looking forward to the visit. Everyone had worked diligently to be prepared during this otherwise very busy time of the year.

It snowed a bit on the way, but we were on schedule. "We need to stop and look at a new sight," I was informed. We pulled off the exit and began to drive around a city none of us had been to before. We parked in a parking lot that allowed us to count the cars passing through the intersection; with every car that passed, so did the time. An hour and a half later, we were back on the road; we were also an hour and a half behind schedule.

As we arrived at the first store, I pulled my boss aside and reminded her we had to stay on track in order to get to the remaining stores. She agreed and we entered the location. I was then informed that we would have to be there for an additional hour or so because of a very important conference call. It was over and I knew it. There would be no way at this point we could visit more than two additional stores and that would be a stretch. How could they not see the lack of respect that was being shown to those managers who were on the front lines for us? The ones who made sure that each day their doors were open. The ones who were making the money to pay for our salaries.

As we entered the car, I was very direct. "We are so behind we will not have time to see most of the other stores." Without giving time for a response, I picked up my phone and began to call the first store manager, informing her that we were delayed and apologizing over and over again. I thanked her and her team for all the work and effort they had put into making sure they were ready, especially during such a busy and stressful time. I wished her a wonderful holiday and asked if she would be so kind as to pass my holiday wishes on to her team. I apologized again and said I looked forward to seeing them after the first of the year. This had not only been a time for my superiors to see the stores, but this was the last time I would be visiting before the holidays and I had hoped to greet everyone myself.

By the second phone call, I began to hear suggestions and ideas coming from the back seat on how we could fix the day, but I continued calling each store with the same long apologetic conversation.

I had been struggling with the notion to leave this company for some time. On that day as I left the last person at the airport,

I made the decision, it was over. This had not been the only time I'd see such a lack of respect for those running our stores. I had spent the past three years finding the daily strength to rise above and it was not worth it anymore. It was time for a change. I knew it and so did those close to me. I am grateful for that day. For me, it was a clear indication as to where the company was going and who was running it. I ran as fast as I could.

Respect flows up and down as well as back and forth. Respect for a manager comes in two forms; respect for the position and respect for the person. When a new manager takes over a store, he quickly sees those who, first of all, respects their title. It is then his task to earn his team's respect.

It doesn't take long to see those who do not respect authority. As a manager, you are the authority. If there are members of your team, whether a new or established team, who do not respect your position, you need to address it quickly. Respect is the first ingredient for developing integrity. Without respect, there is no moral compass. Without respect, one no longer feels it is important to follow rules or policies.

In order for respect to last, the respect for authority must become respect for the person. Careers are very short lived if there is no respect for a superior. Respect for the person is an earned respect. It comes from proving the person is deserving of one's respect.

Respect flows up and down and back and forth, but it always

stops and starts with me. I can respect my boss's position but not respect him as a person. At the same time, I have the power to earn the respect of those who report to me. I control the flow of respect. It may require me to rise above. If I don't respect the decision my company is making or the level of respect shown to those on the front lines, I have the ability to remain respectful and in doing so am respectable. The danger comes when those things that are difficult to respect are unethical. In those situations, respect and stupidity seem to mingle together. It is those situations that need to be addressed with respect but should never be brushed way under the guise of respect.

Here's an example. During a loss prevention conversation, Kathy was asked if she had ever given merchandise away. Kathy, being an honest person, offered that there was a situation when a customer was not charged for an item. She had realized it and had intended to pay for the item out of her own money, but had forgotten. Kathy was terminated for this act.

Kathy was a major player in the store. Removing her, would greatly hinder the store's performance. Kathy's boss – the manager – was not involved in any of the discussion, thus was taken by surprise when told his number one person was no longer with the company.

Action always speaks louder than words, when it comes to respect. In this situation, no one else was brought into the conversation. This proved lack of respect for Kathy. A conversation with the store manager or co-workers would have allowed Kathy's character to be brought into the limelight. The discussion to terminate Kathy was made with no foresight as to how it would affect the store's performance and the team; removing a major player who works 40 hours a week with no warning has great affects.

It is clear that respect for the manager and team was not a part of making the decision to terminate. This is a company who likes to play bad cop, a company that rules by the letter of the law. The manager is now responsible for the respect flow, or lack of it, that is flowing towards him. He can in turn speak out against the company or he can rise above and make as little an issue as possible in order to protect Kathy. After all, it should be up to her if she tells her side of the story or not. The manager also needs to decide how he will address the situation with his superiors, if he so chooses to do so. This manager must also face the fact that his company has little respect for his position and his team, a very sobering fact.

Respect may at times need to be demanded, especially from those who find it difficult to respect anything and anyone. But even in those situations, a manager can quickly turn demanded respect into earned respect. There is an art to earning respect. It is a skill that some are born with and some have to develop. It never happens overnight, it is a process. Once earned, respect becomes a foundation that everything else can be built upon. Earned respect is what allows a team to try harder, reach higher and achieve more. Earned respect turns a staff into a team.

Earned respect comes when honesty, integrity, fairness and trust are established. All four of these characteristics take time to prove.

Honesty: Honesty is seen in the way a manager handles the day to day operations. There is an old saying that who you are, is who you are when no one is looking. The reality is – someone is always looking.

Integrity: Integrity is proven in the way one does his job. It is also proven through conversations. A manager who throws his entire team or one member under the bus to save his own hide, will immediately lose his integrity. A manager who accepts accolades that should be given to his team also falls off the integrity wagon. Once lost, integrity is very difficult to restore.

Fairness: I had a co-worker who said, treating everyone the same isn't treating them fair. Schedules, perfect shifts, favors and favorites are all included in ways that a manager appears fair or unfair.

Trust: Of all four character traits, trust is the hardest to establish. For most people, it takes a very long time to truly trust someone. Once that trust is established, it can be destroyed in a moment. One of the biggest reasons people are untrusting is because of past experiences. You may have an employee who never really trusts you, but if you trust yourself, you will be able to succeed.

The secret of respected managers is that they hold themselves to a very high standard of Honesty, Integrity, Fairness and Trust. They don't need outside approval on these four traits, they know because they judge themselves daily and continually raise their own standards.

# Always Assume

I had the interesting experience of attending a manager's
conference for a company that I had only been employed
with for a short time. Besides the fact I knew next to no one, I
also was still learning about this company, the operations and
overall structure. I am one who enjoys life. I love adventures.
I love being spontaneous. I love parties. HOWEVER, I'm not
sure if adventures, spontaneity and parties should be the
driving forces at a manager's conference. The entire weekend
reflected the pep-rallies we had in high school; complete with
cheerleaders, pompoms and jocks. I did my best to embrace
the adventure but the entire time, I couldn't help but wonder
how this company could possibly survive.

During this strange event, I attended a workshop lead by two young men who were there to offer their wisdom on being a manager. Both looked as if they were two years out of college, and I doubt that either had ever managed anyone in their short careers, and I was sure that if they had, it wasn't in the world of retail or foodservice.

We were given time for discussion within our small groups. As usual, I misinterpreted the questions and had prepared answers that drew confused expressions from those around the table. But, nevertheless, made it through the first half of the workshop. After our break, one of these brilliant young men began the session with three words: Assume Positive Intent. He had my attention. For the next hour, he and his partner spoke about how we are so quick to assume the negative. The phone rings and we wonder what has happened. We see an email from a certain person and we are reluctant to open it assuming the worst. Our boss comes to visit and we are sure we are going to get fired. We walk in on two people talking and immediately think they are talking about us.

Assume Positive Intent – I had never heard such a thing. Assume the good instead of the worst? How odd; yet how different everyday life would be if we all could achieve this. I began observing others in this spotlight and realized that there are very few who assume positive intent; Managers fearful that their next DM visit means termination, Employees certain that the entire company is talking about how bad of an employee they are, co-workers second guessing each other and never being able to take a compliment because they are certain it wasn't intended to be one.

We don't need to change our assumptions, we need to change our entire way of thinking. The world does not revolve around us. The CEO of your company has a great deal of other things to think and talk about besides you and your performance. Rarely does anyone just get fired these days – if someone is coming to terminate your employment, they are coming with a pile of forms you have already signed.

I once shared an office with a marketing manager who was only at her desk one or two days a week. On one particular morning, she informed me that there was a meeting going on in the general manager's office, and she was sure the meeting was all about her and how they were going to fire her. I assured her I didn't think that was the case, but the poor thing sat in fear for two hours while the big meeting was being held in the next office. When the door of the office finally opened, the handful of people exited and informed me that they were going to lunch. She waited through lunch, still certain that this was her last day. From time to time, there would pop up on her computer screen job opportunities in the area, she was making plans. Lunch ended and only the general manager returned. When asked how the meeting went, he responded with a confident, "Great! We're planning next year's budget and things are really solid." There had been no talk of terminations, no discussion around how to get rid of this now anxiety ridden marketing manager. She wasn't even a topic on the list.

If we are always assuming the worst, it reflects in our work. We become argumentative and untrusting; neither qualities found in successful managers. We must learn to assume positive intent, and we must assume that there are those on our team who have not heard of such a thing. There are those who think they are going to be fired, those who think they are always in trouble and those who know for certain that they are the topic of conversation. They are all assuming what is far from positive.

As I sit at the desk writing these words, my phone rings. As usual, I look down at the number. It is not one I recognize. Hmmm, should I answer? Who is on the other end? What do they want? Do I want to have a conversation? I remind myself of those three little words: Assume Positive Intent and answer the phone. It's the doctor's office confirming an appointment in the morning...

# Conformity Can Be a Very Evil Word

There are many very creative individuals in the field of management. There are a plethora of entrepreneurs with no money who have settled into management positions. Then, there are those want-to-be business owners who first feel the need to learn the business before they step out on their own; these are the really bright ones. Creativity in management can be a two-edged sword. Misguided creativity can be disastrous.

Jack was extreme. When it came to humor, he was one of the funniest people I ever encountered, could keep you laughing for hours and did. If it was gossip - he knew more than anyone and as the saying goes, told you more than he knew. Customer service, Jack was the head of the class. Team building, there was nothing that his staff would not and did not do for him. Sales building, Jack could sell you just about anything and have you purchasing several to give to your boss, his secretary and the janitor. On the surface, Jack was the best of the best.

Jack had been in retail for years. According to his resume, he would make his move to a new job every three years. He never made it past store manager but it was not for lack of desire. Jack wanted more than anything to be a district manager, regional manager and why stop there, Jack would have loved to be king.

He had a way of keeping his entire team of people busy without the use of a checklist. Checklists are usually at the heart of all retail and foodservice operations. I have actually seen checklists created to check the checklist for the original checklist. On Jack's shift he was the checklist, continually giving direction, assuring that everyone had a task to do, and everyone was aware of what they needed to begin, as soon as they were finished with the first task.

In the beginning, there were a few issues that needed to be addressed. Jack, obviously, did not like to confront an individual's issue; instead he would make it an entire staff issue and post large warnings in the backroom. At times there could be seven or even eight WARNINGS posted for all to read, in hopes that the one person who had the issue would figure out that they needed to change their behavior. The goal was that the one employee would make those necessary changes on his/her own so Jack would not have to address it personally.

These types of warnings are usually futile. In a small or large staffs, everyone knows who the culprit is, and everyone is wondering why the boss does not address it with that individual instead of making everyone feel as if they are in trouble. The funny thing is that the culprit does not get it and, therefore, thinks the warning must be for someone else, that is, if they even take the time to read the warning in the first place.

Inventory was another problem or *opportunity* – apparently, we are to think that we live in a world where no one has any problems. Creative ordering is what I had been informed Jack called his method. When a manager the caliber of Jack was running a store, taking inventory was a waste of labor. Creative ordering simply required sitting down in front of the computer, guessing what you have on hand and then using that information to decide what additional product was needed. After all the items had been ordered, Jack would confidently hit the submit button and presto - inventory and ordering were completed in minutes. The result was certain, Jack always ran out of what he needed and had more than enough of product he did not need. This resulted in his Backroom requiring more creativity for storage; it is difficult to find room to store items that you really do not need.

Scheduling techniques were also on the questionable list. Why should someone such as Jack be required to use a system that the entire company is required to use, when he could produce a handwritten schedule in a matter of minutes? Sure, there were gaps and labor was not disbursed correctly, and there were always a lot of people working when Jack was scheduled, but all the other times, there were as few as possible. By using a handwritten schedule, it was easier to fix the mistakes later instead of posting an accurate one, which was another directive of the company.

Everything Jack did was creative, fun and had no resemblance to the systems that were required. His store was very profitable, extremely clean, his team loved him and so did the customers. Why in the world would he be expected to conform to company systems when he was so successful doing it his way?

How do you get someone whose entire life is about being different to understand the importance of conforming? Jack was successful using his management style of 'winging it'. How much more successful would he and his store be by using the systems?

After several business reviews, one on ones, and coaching sessions on the importance of using the company systems, I saw little improvement. When Jack was successful in using a system, he would be bouncing off the walls with excitement; this, in turn, gave me hope that someday he would be able to master all of the systems. They were short-lived hopes, it never took more than a few weeks after a success when I would walk into his backroom and find more WARNINGS, or a shelf full of last month's special, and realize we may have won a battle but the war was ongoing.

Jack and I had just finished up a business review. Business reviews were a time when we would look over last month's financial results and make an action plan for those areas that needed improvement, along with discussing any staffing issues and upcoming promotions; a very successful and essential review for any company. During this particular business review, there were several areas that needed improvement. Again, they were not terrible; it was more about how much better they could have been. Jack got up from the table very frustrated. He gathered his papers and started to walk away with his head down.

Still sitting at the table, I called his name rather sternly. He turned around a bit taken back. I told him to sit back down and that we needed to talk. Our talk was definitely a one-sided conversation that went something like this:

Jack, you run a successful store. It is clean and organized. Your team loves you and so do your customers. You are in control of what happens here and there is no doubt in anyone's mind that you are the manager. If I thought that being a store manager was everything you wanted, I would not be pushing you this hard. I know you want more. You want the next promotion and in order to make that a reality, you have to embrace the systems that are in place. If you truly want to be responsible for the operations of eight, ten or even twelve stores, you have to know that they are all using the same system or you will fail.

Jack, what I am asking you to do is conform. I understand that conforming is something you run from, you take pride in your diversity. I know I am asking you do to something far outside your comfort zone. You have to decide if it is worth changing something you hold so dear. You have the ability but you have to decide to accept the company's systems and follow them religiously. I completely understand if you choose not to but you must understand that it has now become a requirement.

If you want the promotion, I will do everything I can to get you ready but I cannot change this for you, you have to make the change.

Jack got up from the table determined to make it work, he wanted to be king more than anything. He made great strides. However, six months later, he decided it was not worth the effort and moved on. Six months after our conversations and almost three years to the day, I had hired him. I am guessing that history was repeating itself.

Wanting to be king and actually becoming king are worlds apart. We all want to be promoted. The only ones who don't are the ones who have experienced it and have come to appreciate the four little walls that enclose their one store. The grass is rarely greener on the other side, if it is greener, it takes much more time and effort to keep it that way. There is definitely a time to break the rules, but you have to know and understand the rules before you can break them.

I recently worked with a company whose systems I felt were flawed. I believed that with a new focus and method, sales would increase greatly. I tested it in one store and the results of the first test were successful. A second store was tested with same results. Prior to testing it, I needed to know and understand how the current system worked, which took time. When I brought up my concern and idea for a new method, there was one simple question asked, "How do we do this and still use our current system?" It was the challenge. Anyone can create a new method, but how you marry the old and new together is important.

Conforming doesn't mean one is giving up or giving in. It means that one has agreed to work within the current system opposed to standing on the outside screaming for change. One can more effectively create change when one is inside.

It takes an Entrepreneur's mentality to design ways to improve the current system and it takes creativity to marry the new and old together.

*Side note: Jack is now a very successful District Manager for a very large company. He is making changes and impacting his co-workers daily. Last I heard, he is training others on how to do it RIGHT!*

# Interpersonal Skills

Twenty years ago we called this a team player. Back then, you couldn't get a degree in team playing, today you can get one in Interpersonal Relationships.

Here are some random definitions of Interpersonal Skills:

- Works effectively with others

- Establishes and maintains good working relationships

- Adheres to the team's expectations, responsibilities and guidelines

- Is seen as a team player and is cooperative

- Assists others to achieve their goals

- Does what's right ethically

- Builds rapport

- Helps people feel valued, appreciated and included in discussions

- Relates well to others

- Interacts well with people at all levels, is easy to approach and talk to, is a good listener

- Uses diplomacy and tact

- Is open to new ideas

- Listens to others objectively

- Is respectful

- Uses language and behavior that reflects and enhances the dignity of diverse customers and co-workers

- Makes a positive contribution

- Shares information, listens and accepts others' points of view

- Able to give and receive constructive feedback

We could all agree that these are the kind of people we want on our teams. Tell me where they hang out and I'll go hire a few. But we are talking about our own personal style. How well do you measure up? Do you see yourself on this list? Does it describe you? Are you a team player?

There are managers who exemplify the "Do as I say, not as I do" concept. They hold high expectations for those who report to them and those who they report to; however, their personal expectations are backed with excuses why they can't achieve, hit goals or get things done.

Interpersonal Skill is just that – PERSONAL. These do define you. They are within your control. They are the building blocks for honesty, integrity, respect and trust. They determine if you qualify as a team player.

# Perception Is Reality, But Reality Isn't Always Perception

Many management books and company training material will say that Perception is Reality. What is meant by this is that what our employees perceive, becomes their reality. If they perceive that getting tasks done is more important than taking care of customers, their reality will be to focus on the tasks and not the customer.

Perception comes from past experience. If a manager does not communicate properly nor set clear expectations, an employee is forced to rely on their past experiences to understand present circumstances. For example, if an employee is used to having monthly one on ones with their manager and finds themselves working for someone who never communicates how they are doing, she will begin to think that she is failing or that the manager doesn't like her. Her perception is her reality.

As a manager, it is important to understand this concept, but even more important is to understand that reality isn't always perception. We, in many ways, are no different than our employees. We perceive things within our company, or from our boss that we allow to become our reality. When, in fact, it may only be our perception. Mangers must learn to live on both sides of this statement. Understanding that our employee's reality is their perception, but ours must not be. Perception is reality, but reality isn't always perception.

# Conclusion

Retail is defined as the sale of goods to the public for use or consumption. It is reported that 65 – 70% of our nation's Gross Domestic Product comes from retail. Although online shopping has changed the way we do business, 90% of retail sales are done in-store. For each store there exists a manager.

There is a multitude of books written on business, leadership and management, however, most of them target the corporate environment. Although it is challenging to build a team and execute company directives in any situation, managing in the presence of the general public or *the customer* redefines the term complex. This combined with the reality that the majority of retail/food service employees are temporary, provides a Retail Manager with an endless supply of challenges.

The position of Manager can no longer be held by just anyone; to execute this role properly requires skill, knowledge and talent. I will admit that there was once a time I believed anyone could do this job. I looked at it as the bridge job, the one you do until the real job comes along. I see now that I was wrong in this assumption. Not everyone can do this job and even fewer can do it well.

Management takes stamina, creativity, intelligence and determination. It can be very lonely at times and at others times, you just want to lock the front doors for a few hours of peace and quiet. It's a job that demands all your attention one day and the next day can bore you to death. It's a job that rates you equal to the day's sales and starts with a clean slate the next morning. On it's best day, it's a rush and on it's worst it can be devastating – but there's always tomorrow.

I have learned to love my little shops, whether they are 1200 square foot boutiques or 20,000 square foot boxes. I am the merchant who has something others want to purchase and I make that happen. I give people jobs and teach them skills that will not only benefit my business but their lives. I get to interact with total strangers all day long and have the chance to make them friends. I set goals that seem unattainable and when achieved, dance merrily around the store. I've been known to give mannequins names and tell them secrets. I'm the first to taste the newest bakery item before the customer. I create, serve, sell. I am a manager.

## The Retail Ladder

A community of managers sharing lessons, successes and great stories. We invite you to join the conversation!

**www.theretailladder.com**

Future Publications in the *Lessons Learned in Retail Management Series:*

>Vol 2: The Best ADVISE I ever got!

>Vol 3: A Funny Thing Happened on the Way to the Register

*The Best ADVISE I ever got!* and *A Funny Thing Happened on the Way to the Register* are collections of stories from real Retail Managers. To find out more and submit your own stories, visit www.theretailladder.coom

Join the Retail Manager Group on Facebook:

>The Retail Ladder

## Jeannie G Bruenning

A Chicago transplant, Jeannie and husband Jeff currently enjoy life on California's Central Coast. Wife, mother and grand-mother; Jeannie added author and publisher to the list in 2009. She serves on the board of SLONightWriters, a local non-profit writing group. A *Forever Retail Manager,* Jeannie stays involved in the retail world developing and coaching fellow retail managers and serving customers.

www.jeanniegb.com

www.ingramcontent.com/pod-product-compliance
Lightning Source LLC
Chambersburg PA
CBHW021922190326
41519CB00009B/880